On Generating the Resolve
To Become a Buddha

The publication of this book has been enabled by
a generous donation from Upāsaka Guo Ke.

The publication of this book has been enabled by
a generous donation from Upāsaka Guo Ke.

A Note on the Proper Care of Dharma Materials

Traditional Buddhist cultures treat books on Dharma as sacred. Hence it is considered disrespectful to place them in a low position, to read them when lying down, or to place them where they might be damaged by food or drink.

ON GENERATING THE RESOLVE TO BECOME A BUDDHA

Three Classic Texts on the Bodhisattva Vow:

On Generating the Resolve to Become a Buddha
Chapter Six of Ārya Nāgārjuna's *Ten Grounds Vibhāṣā*

Exhortation to Resolve on Buddhahood
By the Dhyāna Master and Pureland Patriarch, Shixian

Exhortation to Resolve on Buddhahood
By the Tang Dynasty Literatus, Peixiu

Translation by Bhikshu Dharmamitra

KALAVINKA PRESS
Seattle, Washington
WWW.KALAVINKAPRESS.ORG

KALAVINKA PRESS
8603 39th Ave SW
Seattle, WA 98136 USA

WWW.KALAVINKAPRESS.ORG / WWW.KALAVINKA.ORG

Kalavinka Press is associated with the Kalavinka Dharma Association, a non-profit organized exclusively for religious educational purposes as allowed within the meaning of section 501(c)3 of the Internal Revenue Code. Kalavinka Dharma Association was founded in 1990 and gained formal approval in 2004 by the United States Internal Revenue Service as a 501(c)3 non-profit organization to which all donations are tax deductible.

Donations to KDA are accepted by mail and on the Kalavinka website where numerous free Dharma translations and excerpts from Kalavinka publications are available in digital format.

Edition: Bcitta-SA-1008-1.0
© 2005–2009 Bhikshu Dharmamitra
ISBN: 978-1-935413-08-0
Library of Congress Control Number: 2009920876

PUBLISHER'S CATALOGING-IN-PUBLICATION DATA

Nagarjuna, Shixian, Peixiu.

On Generating the Resolve to Become a Buddha. Three Classic Works Encouraging the Resolve to Pursue the Bodhisattva Path to Buddhahood. Translations by Bhikshu Dharmamitra. – 1st ed. – Seattle, WA: Kalavinka Press, 2009.

p. ; cm.
ISBN: 978-1-935413-08-0
Includes: Text outline; facing-page Chinese source text in both traditional and simplified scripts; notes.
Other authors: Nagarjuna, 2nd c.; Shixian, 1686–1734; Peixiu, 797–870; Zongmi, 780–840.

1. Bodhicitta (Buddhism). 2. Compassion—Religious aspects—Buddhism. 3. Bodhisattvas. 4. Spiritual life —Mahayana Buddhism. I. Shi zhu piposha lun. II. On Generating the Resolve to Become a Buddha. III. Exhortation to Resolve on Buddhahood. IV. Title.

2009920876
0902

Cover and interior designed and composed by Bhikshu Dharmamitra.

ON GENERATING THE RESOLVE
TO BECOME A BUDDHA

Three Classic Texts on the Bodhisattva Vow:

On Generating the Resolve to Become a Buddha
Chapter Six of Ārya Nāgārjuna's *Ten Grounds Vibhāṣā*

Exhortation to Resolve on Buddhahood
By the Dhyāna Master and Pureland Patriarch, Shixian

Exhortation to Resolve on Buddhahood
By the Tang Dynasty Literatus, Peixiu

Translation by Bhikshu Dharmamitra

KALAVINKA PRESS
Seattle, Washington
WWW.KALAVINKAPRESS.ORG

KALAVINKA PRESS
8603 39th Ave SW
Seattle, WA 98136 USA

WWW.KALAVINKAPRESS.ORG / WWW.KALAVINKA.ORG

Kalavinka Press is associated with the Kalavinka Dharma Association, a non-profit organized exclusively for religious educational purposes as allowed within the meaning of section 501(c)3 of the Internal Revenue Code. Kalavinka Dharma Association was founded in 1990 and gained formal approval in 2004 by the United States Internal Revenue Service as a 501(c)3 non-profit organization to which all donations are tax deductible.

Donations to KDA are accepted by mail and on the Kalavinka website where numerous free Dharma translations and excerpts from Kalavinka publications are available in digital format.

Edition: Bcitta-SA-1008-1.0
© 2005–2009 Bhikshu Dharmamitra
ISBN: 978-1-935413-08-0
Library of Congress Control Number: 2009920876

PUBLISHER'S CATALOGING-IN-PUBLICATION DATA

Nagarjuna, Shixian, Peixiu.

On Generating the Resolve to Become a Buddha. Three Classic Works Encouraging the Resolve to Pursue the Bodhisattva Path to Buddhahood. Translations by Bhikshu Dharmamitra. – 1st ed. – Seattle, WA: Kalavinka Press, 2009.

p. ; cm.
ISBN: 978-1-935413-08-0
Includes: Text outline; facing-page Chinese source text in both traditional and simplified scripts; notes.
Other authors: Nagarjuna, 2nd c.; Shixian, 1686–1734; Peixiu, 797–870; Zongmi, 780–840.

1. Bodhicitta (Buddhism). 2. Compassion—Religious aspects—Buddhism. 3. Bodhisattvas. 4. Spiritual life —Mahayana Buddhism. I. Shi zhu piposha lun. II. On Generating the Resolve to Become a Buddha. III. Exhortation to Resolve on Buddhahood. IV. Title.

2009920876
0902

Cover and interior designed and composed by Bhikshu Dharmamitra.

Dedicated to the memory of the selfless and marvelous life of the Venerable Dhyāna Master Hsuan Hua, the Weiyang Ch'an Patriarch and the very personification of the Bodhisattva Path.

DHYĀNA MASTER HSUAN HUA

宣化禪師

1918–1995

About the Chinese Text

This translation is supplemented by inclusion of Chinese source text on verso pages in both traditional and simplified scripts. Taisho-supplied variant readings from other editions are presented as Chinese endnotes.

This Chinese text and its variant readings are from the Chinese Buddhist Electronic Text Association's digital edition of the Taisho compilation of the Buddhist canon.

Those following the translation in the Chinese should be aware that Taisho scripture punctuation is not traceable to original editions, is often erroneous and misleading, and is probably best ignored altogether. (In any case, accurate reading of Classical Chinese does not require any punctuation at all.)

Outlining in This Work:

Unless otherwise noted, nearly all of the outline headings in Kalavinka Press translations originate with the translator. Buddhist canonical writings are often so metaphysically profound and structurally dense that they are best attended by detailed outline headings to facilitate understanding of the text.

Citation and Romanization Protocols

Kalavinka Press *Taisho* citation style adds text numbers after volume numbers and before page numbers to assist rapid digital searches. Romanization, where used, is Pinyin with the exception of names and terms already well-recognized in Wade-Giles romanization.

General Table of Contents

ACKNOWLEDGMENTS

The accuracy and readability of these first ten books of translations have been significantly improved with the aid of extensive corrections, preview comments, and editorial suggestions generously contributed by Bhikkhu Bodhi, Jon Babcock, Upāsaka Feng Ling, Upāsaka Guo Ke, Timothy J. Lenz, and Richard Robinson. Additional valuable editorial suggestions and corrections were offered by Bhikshu Huifeng, Upāsikā Min Li, and Bruce Munson.

The publication of the initial set of ten translation volumes has been assisted by substantial donations to the Kalavinka Dharma Association by Bill and Peggy Brevoort, Freda Chen, David Fox, Upāsaka Guo Ke, Chenping and Luther Liu, Sunny Lou, Jimi Neal, and "Leo L." (a.k.a. *Camellia sinensis folium*). Additional helpful donations were offered by Doug Adams, Diane Hodgman, Joel and Amy Lupro, Richard Robinson, Ching Smith, and Sally and Ian Timm.

Were it not for the ongoing material support provided by my late guru's Dharma Realm Buddhist Association and the serene translation studio provided by Seattle's Bodhi Dhamma Center, creation of this translation would have been immensely more difficult.

Most importantly, it would have been impossible for me to produce this translation without the Dharma teachings provided by my late guru, the Weiyang Ch'an Patriarch, Dharma teacher, and exegete, the Venerable Master Hsuan Hua.

TRANSLATOR'S INTRODUCTION

I present in this volume translations of three classic authoritative works (one by a well-known Indian Buddhist patriarch, and two by famous Chinese Buddhist authors) on the bodhisattva's altruistically-motivated resolve to realize the utmost, right, and perfect enlightenment of a buddha. These three texts are intended as a complement to my translation of Vasubandhu's *Treatise on Resolving to Become a Buddha* which I am publishing under separate cover. These four works, in aggregate, are essential foundational components in a series of works I have translated by Ārya Nāgārjuna and other Mahāyāna eminences on the doctrinal underpinnings and precise practice terrains of the Bodhisattva Path.

My motivation in translating these works devoted to the bodhisattva's vow, the bodhisattva's practice, and the bodhisattva's multi-lifetime path has been to make at least some small contribution to the development of an enhanced understanding of Buddhism on the part of those many people in the West who self-identify as "Buddhist," but who may not possess a clear idea of what Shākyamuni Buddha intended by the path to the cessation of suffering, whether that path is aimed at individual liberation (as in modern Theravada practice) or whether it aspires to universal liberation (as with the Mahāyāna).

It has been my perception for some time now that Westerners of refined spiritual intelligence and aptitude are readily attracted to the Buddhist ideals of giving, moral virtue, patience, vigorous pursuit of goodness, meditative serenity, wisdom, and compassion. That is, of course, all well and good, for pursuing them will certainly create a more spiritually meaningful, happy, and satisfying life. That said, unless such altruism, idealism, and meditative practice are conjoined with a lucid understanding of the path to spiritual liberation, there is not likely to be any enduringly useful result which will ensue in subsequent lifetimes. Hence the need to develop a more refined understanding of the Path. We are fortunate to live in a time when a flood of new scriptural translation and interpretation is becoming available in the West from both within the tradition and without. I hope this small volume may serve as a useful complement to the materials already available.

The author of the first very short text on bodhi resolve should need no introduction. Ārya Nāgārjuna, who probably lived sometime during the second century of the common era, was one of the most influential monks in the propagation of the Mahāyāna universal-liberation path. The text presented here is the sixth chapter of his commentary on the ten stages of the Bodhisattva Path (*daśabhūmika-vibhāṣā*).

The second work in this book is probably the most popular and deeply moving of all currently extant exhortations to bodhi resolve contained in the Chinese Buddhist canon. Its author, a famous Qing Dynasty monk, pureland patriarch, and meditation master by the name of Sheng'an Shixian (pronounced by many modern Chinese as "Xing'an Shixian") has, through this exhortation, stirred many Buddhists to deep faith in the Bodhisattva Path. My own guru, Master Hsuan Hua, delivered a series of Dharma lectures on this work. His lecture-series commentary, entitled *Exhortation to Resolve Upon Bodhi*, was translated and published by the Buddhist Text Translation Society in 2003.

The third and final work in this book is a stirring bodhi-resolve exhortation by Peixiu, an eminent literatus and Dharma friend of the famous Tang Dynasty patriarch, exegete, and meditation master, Zongmi (whose preface to that work I have included herein). Incidentally, Peixiu, also well-known for his interactions with famous Ch'an masters, eventually rose to become prime minister in the Tang Dynasty capital.

A brief note on the outlining found in these translations: In the case of the chapter from Ārya Nāgārjuna's ten stages commentary, all outlining originates with the English translator. In the case of the Peixiu exhortation, the primary chapter titles originate with the Chinese text. The more detailed outlining was added by the translator. In the case of the Qing Dynasty text by the Venerable Patriarch Sheng'an Shixian, that outlining originates almost entirely from the commentary by the famous and learned early twentieth century mainland monk, the Venerable Yuanying.

It is my hope that reading these translations of bodhi-resolve texts may inspire deeply reflective English Dharma readers to develop, cherish, and sustain the most noble of aspirations.

Bhikshu Dharmamitra
Seattle
November 1, 2008

Part One:

ON GENERATING THE RESOLVE TO BECOME A BUDDHA

Ārya Nāgārjuna's *Ten Grounds Vibhāṣā* – Chapter. 6

Part One Contents

ON GENERATING THE RESOLVE TO BECOME A BUDDHA

发菩提心品第六。

[35a23] 问曰。初发心是诸愿根本。云何为初发心。答曰。

初发菩提心。或三四因缘。

[35a26] 众生初发菩提心。或以三因缘。或以四因缘。如是和合有七因缘。发阿耨多罗三藐三菩提心。问曰。何等为七。答曰。

一者诸如来。令发菩提心。
二见法欲坏。守护故发心。

三于众生中。大悲而发心。
四或有菩萨。教发菩提心。

五见菩萨行。亦随而发心。
或因布施已。而发菩提心。

或见佛身相。欢喜而发心。
以是七因缘。而发菩提心。

[35b08] 佛令发心者。佛以佛眼观众生。知其善根淳熟堪任能得阿耨多罗三藐三菩提。如是人者。

简体字

發菩提心品第六。

[35a23] 問曰。初發心是諸願根本。云何為初發心。答曰。

初發菩提心。或三四因緣。

[35a26] 眾生初發菩提心。或以三因緣。或以四因緣。如是和合有七因緣。發阿耨多羅三藐三菩提心。問曰。何等為七。答曰。

一者諸如來。令發菩提心。
二見法欲壞。守護故發心。

三於眾生中。大悲而發心。
四或有菩薩。教發菩提心。

五見菩薩行。亦隨而發心。
或因布施已。而發菩提心。

或見佛身相。歡喜而發心。
以是七因緣。而發菩提心。

[35b08] 佛令發心者。佛以佛眼觀眾生。知其善根淳熟堪任能得阿耨多羅三藐三菩提。如是人者。

正體字

On Generating the Resolve to Become a Buddha[1]
By Ārya Nāgārjuna

Question: The initial generation of the resolve [to realize buddhahood] is the root of all vows. What then is meant by this "initial generation of resolve"?

Response:

The initial resolve to realize bodhi
May involve three or four types of causes and conditions.

When beings initially generate the resolve to realize bodhi, it may find its origin in a set of three causal bases or else in a set of four causal bases. Thus, when one combines them, one has a total of seven causes and conditions associated with generating the resolve to gain *anuttara-samyak-saṃbodhi*.

Question: What then are those seven?

Response:

In the case of the first, the Tathāgatas
May influence one to generate the resolve to realize bodhi.
Second, observing that the Dharma is on the verge of destruction,
One generates the resolve in order to guard and protect it.

In the case of the third, when in the midst of beings,
One feels compassion for them and therefore initiates the resolve.
As for the fourth, one may have a bodhisattva
Instruct one in generation of the resolve to realize bodhi.

Fifth, one may observe the conduct of a bodhisattva
And, in emulating him, one may generate the resolve.
Or alternatively, in the aftermath of an act of giving,
One may generate the resolve to realize bodhi based on that.

Or else, on seeing the characteristic signs of a buddha's body,
One may feel delight and then proceed to generate the resolve.
Thus it may be on account of seven causes and conditions
That one generates the resolve to realize bodhi.

A.   THE INFLUENCE OF A BUDDHA

As for a buddha influencing one to generate the resolve, the Buddha employs the buddha eye to observe beings. He may then realize that a person's roots of goodness have become so completely ripe that he is capable of taking on this endeavor and will be able to realize *anuttara-samyak-saṃbodhi*. In the case of a person of this sort, the

佛教令发心作是言。善男子
来。今可发心当度苦恼众
生。或复有人生在恶世。见
法欲坏。为守护故。发心作
是念。咄哉从无量无边百千
万亿阿僧只劫来。唯有一人
二处行出三界。四圣谛大导
师。知五种法藏脱于六道。
有七种正法大宝。深行八解
脱。以九部经教化。有十大
力说十一种功德。善转十二
因缘相续。说十三助圣道
法。有十四觉意大宝。除十
五种贪欲。并得十六心无碍
解脱。

佛教令發心作是言。善男子
來。今可發心當度苦惱眾
生。或復有人生在惡世。見
法欲壞。為守護故。發心作
是念。咄哉從無量無邊百千
萬億阿僧祇劫來。唯有一人
二處行出三界。四聖諦大導
師。知五種法藏脫於六道。
有七種正法大寶。深行八解
脫。以九部經教化。有十大
力說十一種功德。善轉十二
因緣相續。說十三助聖道
法。有十四覺意大寶。除十
五種貪欲。并得十六心無礙
解脫。

简体字   正體字

Buddha instructs him and causes him to generate the resolve, saying to him, "Son of good family, come forth. You are now capable of bringing forth the resolve to liberate beings from suffering and affliction."

B. THE MOTIVATION TO PROTECT THE DHARMA

Or then again there may be persons born into a dreadful era who, on observing that the Dharma is about to meet its destruction, generate the aspiration out of the motivation to preserve the Dharma, and thus contemplate in the following way:

Alas! From a time an immeasurable and boundless number of hundreds of thousands of myriads of *koṭīs* of *asaṃkhyeyas* of kalpas ago on forth to the very present, there has only been:

— A single person,
— On two bases,
— Who has moved forth into the three realms,
— Who has served as the great guiding guru of the four truths of the Ārya,
— Who is that one who has known the five-fold treasury of Dharma,
— Who has gained liberation from the six destinies of rebirth,
— Who has possessed the great jewel of the seven kinds of right Dharma,
— Who has deeply practiced the eight liberations,
— Who has employed the nine categories of sutra text in teaching and transformation,
— Who has gained possession of the ten great powers,
— Who has described the eleven kinds of meritorious qualities,
— Who has skillfully set forth the continuous cycle of the twelve causes and conditions,
— Who has explained the thirteen types of dharmas assisting realization of the Path of the Āryas,[2]
— Who has possessed the great jewel of the fourteen factors fundamental to awakening,
— Who has gotten rid of the fifteen kinds of craving,
— Who has gained realization of the sixteen mind states involved in the uninterrupted path (*ānantarya-mārga*) and the path of liberation (*vimukti-mārga*),

出十六地狱众生。及身十七
具足十八不共法。善分别十
九住果人。善知分别学人阿
罗汉辟支佛诸佛二十根是。
大悲心者。是大将主大众主
大医王大导师大船师。久乃
得是法。行难行苦行。乃得
是法。而今欲坏。我当发阿
耨多罗三藐三菩提心。厚种
善根得成佛道。令法久住无
数阿僧只劫。又行菩萨道
时。护持无量诸佛法故勤行
精进。或复有人见众生苦
恼。可愍无救无归无所依
止。流转生死险难恶道。有
大怨贼诸恶虫兽生死恐怖诸
恶鬼等。

出十六地獄眾生。及身十七
具足十八不共法。善分別十
九住果人。善知分別學人阿
羅漢辟支佛諸佛二十根是。
大悲心者。是大將主大眾主
大醫王大導師大船師。久乃
得是法。行難行苦行。乃得
是法。而今欲壞。我當發阿
耨多羅三藐三菩提心。厚種
善根得成佛道。令法久住無
數阿僧祇劫。又行菩薩道
時。護持無量諸佛法故勤行
精進。或復有人見眾生苦
惱。可愍無救無歸無所依
止。流轉生死險難惡道。有
大怨賊諸惡虫獸生死恐怖諸
惡鬼等。

简体字　　　　　　　　　　　　正體字

— Who has extricated beings from sixteen kinds of hells,
— Who has also mastered the seventeen physical dharmas,[3]
— Who has completely perfected the eighteen dharmas exclusive [to the Buddhas],
— Who has skillfully distinguished the nineteen stations of persons who have gained the fruits [of the Path],
— And who has known well and distinguished clearly the twenty kinds of roots of those still in training, of the arhats, of the pratyekabuddhas, and of all buddhas.

This one possessed of the mind of great compassion, this great lord of generals, the lord of the Great Assembly, this king of the great physicians, this great guide, this great captain of the ship—over the course of a very long time then and only then succeeded in gaining this Dharma.

He cultivated those ascetic practices so difficult to practice and only then succeeded in gaining this Dharma. But now, it is on the verge of meeting its destruction. I should generate the resolve to gain *anuttara-samyak-saṃbodhi*, should plant thick roots of goodness, should thus gain realization of the path to buddhahood, and thus should cause the Dharma to abide for a long time, enduring even for countless *asaṃkhyeyas* of kalpas.

[Of this same sort are those who], while cultivating the Bodhisattva Path, strive with diligence and vigor to guard and uphold the Dharma of the incalculably many Buddhas.

C. COMPASSION FOR THE SUFFERING OF BEINGS

Or, alternately, there may be persons who observe:

— That beings, beset as they are by bitter afflictions, are to be pitied,
— That they have no one to rescue them, no one in whom to take refuge, and no one on whom they can rely,
— That they flow along in the dangers and difficulties of cyclic birth-and-death, risking descent into the wretched destinies,
— That they are afflicted by great adversaries and insurgents, by all manner of fearsome insects and animals, by the terrors involved in births and deaths, by all manner of fearsome ghosts, and by other circumstances as well,

常有忧悲苦恼刺蕀。恩爱别
离怨会深坑。喜乐之水甚为
难得。大寒大热独行其中。
旷绝无荫难得度脱。众生于
中多诸怖畏。无有救护将导
之者。见如是众生。入此生
死险恶道中受诸苦恼。以大
悲故发阿耨多罗三藐三菩
提心。作是言。我当为无救
作救无归作归无依作依。
我得度已当度众生。我得
脱已当脱众生。我得安已当
安众生。复有人但从人闻以
信乐心等。发无上道心。作
是念。我[3]当修善法不断绝
故。或堕必定得无生法忍。

常有憂悲苦惱刺蕀。恩愛別
離怨會深坑。喜樂之水甚為
難得。大寒大熱獨行其中。
曠絕無蔭難得度脫。眾生於
中多諸怖畏。無有救護將導
之者。見如是眾生。入此生
死險惡道中受諸苦惱。以大
悲故發阿耨多羅三藐三菩提
心。作是言。我當為無救作
救無歸作歸無依作依。我得
度已當度眾生。我得脫已當
脫眾生。我得安已當安眾
生。復有人但從人聞以信
樂心等。發無上道心。作
是念。我[3]當修善法不斷絕
故。或墮必定得無生法忍。

简体字   正體字

— That they are constantly pierced by the thorns of the sufferings and afflictions from worry and sadness,
— That they fall into the deep pit of [sufferings associated
with] separation from those they love and proximity to
those they detest,
— That the waters of joy and happiness are only very rarely
encountered,
— That they travel alone in the midst of intense cold and
intense heat,
— That they are stranded without shade in the vast wilderness and find it difficult to make their way across to
liberation,
— That beings in the midst of all of this are possessed by all
manner of terror and fearfulness,
— And that they have no one to rescue them or serve as
guides for them.

Having observed that beings have entered in this manner into the
dangerous and wretched destinies involved in cyclic births and
deaths and undergo all manner of suffering and affliction, such a
person, on account of the great compassion, may then generate for
their sakes the resolve to gain the realization of *anuttara-samyak-
saṃbodhi* and may then proclaim: "I shall become a rescuer for those
who have no one to rescue them. I shall become a refuge for those
who have no one in whom to take refuge. I will become one upon
whom those with no one to rely on may then rely.

"Once I have succeeded in making my way across, I shall
endeavor to bring beings on across as well. Once I have gained liberation, I shall then liberate these beings as well. Once I have succeeded in gaining peace, I shall see that beings are then established
in peacefulness as well."

D. The Instructive Influence of a Bodhisattva

Then again, there are also those who need only hear of this matter
from others to be inspired to thoughts imbued with faith and happiness, whereupon they generate the resolve to gain realization of the
unsurpassed path. They think, "I should cultivate wholesome dharmas." Now, t could occur that, on account of unremitting practice,
[in the absence of timely and appropriate instruction], they might
fall down into the [arhat path's] "right and fixed position" (*samyak-
tva niyāma*) on realizing the unproduced-dharmas patience.[4]

集诸[4]福德善根淳熟故。或
值诸佛或值大菩萨。能知众
生诸根利钝深心本末性欲差
别。善知方便为般若波罗蜜
所护。能作佛事者知我发
愿。善根成熟故令住必定。
若无生[5]法忍。是诸菩萨。
在第七第八第九第十地。如
佛善知众生心力教令发心。
不以但有信乐力等教令发
心。复有人见馀菩萨行道修
诸善根大悲所护。具足方便
教化众生。不惜身命多所利
益。广博多闻世间奇特人中
标胜。

集諸[4]福德善根淳熟故。或
值諸佛或值大菩薩。能知眾
生諸根利鈍深心本末性欲差
別。善知方便為般若波羅蜜
所護。能作佛事者知我發
願。善根成熟故令住必定。
若無生[5]法忍。是諸菩薩。
在第七第八第九第十地。如
佛善知眾生心力教令發心。
不以但有信樂力等教令發
心。復有人見餘菩薩行道修
諸善根大悲所護。具足方便
教化眾生。不惜身命多所利
益。廣博多聞世間奇特人中
標勝。

简体字　　　　　　　　　　　　　正體字

But on account of accumulating all manner of merit and roots of goodness which have become thoroughly ripened, they may then be able to encounter a buddha, or else may be able to encounter a great bodhisattva, one of those beings who is able to know the sharpness and dullness of the faculties of beings, is able to know from root to branch the deepest thoughts of beings, is able to know the distinctions existing in their natures and desires, is able to well understand what constitutes appropriate skillful means, and who is protected by the Prajñāpāramitā.

Those [beings of this sort] who are able to carry on the works of a Buddha will realize when we have generated the vow. Then, on account of our ripening roots of goodness, they may then cause us to abide in [the Bodhisattva Path's] "right and fixed position" upon realizing the unproduced-dharmas patience.[5] These bodhisattvas are those abiding on the seventh, eighth, ninth, or tenth bodhisattva grounds. In a manner comparable to that of the Buddha, they skill-fully assess the mental powers of individual beings and instruct them accordingly, causing them to bring forth the resolve.

In a case such as this, [success in this matter] is not solely on account of such things as the power of faith and happiness [occur-ring on hearing of the great matter], but rather is a case of being taught [by such great beings] to generate the resolve [to strive for buddhahood].

E. The Aspiration to Emulate the Conduct of Bodhisattvas

Yet again, there are those persons who observe other bodhisattvas in their coursing along on the Path. They observe them as they cul-tivate all manner of roots of goodness and as they proceed along under the protection of the great compassion. [They observe those bodhisattvas in] their perfecting of appropriate skillful means and in their teaching and transforming of beings. [They observe]:

— That, as they accomplish an abundance of beneficial deeds, they refrain from indulging any cherishing re-gard for their own bodies or lives,
— That they become vast in the extensiveness of their learning,
— That they become the most especially distinctive persons in the world,
— That they become the most emblematic among people in their superiority,

疲苦众生为作荫覆。安住布施持戒忍辱精进禅定智慧惭愧质直柔软调和。其心清净深乐善法。见如是人而作是念。是人所行我亦应行所修愿行我亦应修。我为得是法故当发是愿。作是念已发无上道心。复有人行大布施。施佛及僧或但施佛以饮食衣服等。是人因是布施。念过去诸菩萨能行施者。韦蓝摩韦首多罗萨婆檀尸毗王等。即发菩提心。以此施福迴向阿耨多罗三藐三菩提。复有人若见若闻佛三十二相。足下平．手足轮．指网缦．手足柔软．七处满．纤长指．足跟广．身佣直．	疲苦眾生為作蔭覆。安住布施持戒忍辱精進禪定智慧慚愧質直柔軟調和。其心清淨深樂善法。見如是人而作是念。是人所行我亦應行所修願行我亦應修。我為得是法故當發是願。作是念已發無上道心。復有人行大布施。施佛及僧或但施佛以飲食衣服等。是人因是布施。念過去諸菩薩能行施者。韋藍摩韋首多羅薩婆檀尸毗王等。即發菩提心。以此施福迴向阿耨多羅三藐三菩提。復有人若見若聞佛三十二相。足下平．手足輪．指網縵．手足柔軟．七處滿．纖長指．足跟廣．身傭直．
简体字	正體字

— That they serve as a source of shade for those beings who have become weary and afflicted by suffering,
— That they become established in the practices of giving, of moral virtue, of patience, of vigor, of dhyāna absorption, of wisdom, of a sense of shame, of a sense of blame, of straightforwardness in character, of mental pliancy, and of self regulation,
— That their minds are pure,
— And that they are profoundly delighted by coursing in good dharmas.

On observing persons such as these they are inspired to reflect, "I, too, should course in those practices coursed in by these men. I, too, should cultivate just such vows and conduct as they themselves do practice. I should generate this vow for the sake of realizing this Dharma." Having had this thought, they then proceed to generate the resolve to realize the unsurpassed path.

F. Inspiration Provoked by an Act of Giving

Yet again, there are those persons who engage in acts of great giving, acts wherein they present gifts to a buddha or to his sangha, or who may merely make a gift of food, drink, or robes to a buddha. On account of such acts of giving, these persons may call to mind those bodhisattvas of the past who were able to course in giving, such bodhisattvas as Velāma, Vessantara,[6] Sarvada, and King Śibi. [Having called them to mind], they may then straightaway generate the resolve to gain the realization of bodhi and thus may proceed with dedicating the merit from their giving to *anuttara-samyak-sambodhi*.

G. Inspiration Arising from Observing a Buddha's Physical Features

Yet again, there may be those persons who directly observe or merely hear about the thirty-two marks of the Buddhas, namely such marks as:

— The evenness of their soles,
— The wheel-marks on the hands and feet,
— The webbing at the roots of their fingers,
— The softness of their hands and feet,
— The fullness in seven places,
— The slenderness and length of their fingers,
— The breadth of their heels,
— The straightness of their bodies,

足跌高平．毛上旋．伊泥[跳-兆+専]．臂长过膝．阴马藏．身金色．皮软薄．一一孔一毛生．眉间白毫．上身如师子．肩圆大．腋下满．得知妙味．身方如尼拘楼陀树．顶有肉髻．广长舌．梵音声．师子颊．四十齿．齐白密致．眼睛绀青色．睫如牛王等相。心则欢喜作是念。我亦当得如是相。如是相人所得诸法我亦当得。即发阿耨多罗三藐三菩提心。以是七因缘发菩提心。问曰。汝说七因缘发菩萨心。为皆当成有成有不成。答曰。是不必尽成。或有成有不成。

足跌高平．毛上旋．伊泥[跳-兆+専]．臂長過膝．陰馬藏．身金色．皮軟薄．一一孔一毛生．眉間白毫．上身如師子．肩圓大．腋下滿．得知妙味．身方如尼拘樓陀樹．頂有肉髻．廣長舌．梵音聲．師子頰．四十齒．齊白密緻．眼睛紺青色．睫如牛王等相。心則歡喜作是念。我亦當得如是相。如是相人所得諸法我亦當得。即發阿耨多羅三藐三菩提心。以是七因緣發菩提心。問曰。汝說七因緣發菩薩心。為皆當成有成有不成。答曰。是不必盡成。或有成有不成。

简体字   正體字

— Their high and even ankles,
— The upward-pointing and swirling of their bodily hairs,
— Their shanks resembling those of the *aiṇeya* antelope,
— Their arms whereby the fingers reach below the knees,
— Their genital ensheathment like that of a stallion,
— The gold color of their bodies,
— The softness and thinness of their skin,
— The placement of but a single hair in each pore,
— Their white "hair-mark" betwixt their brows,
— Their lion-like bodies,
— Their round and large shoulders,
— The fullness of the axillary region,
— Their ability to distinctly know sublime flavors,
— Their physical girth like that of the *nyagrodha* tree,
— Their flesh-cowl atop the crown of their heads,
— Their vast and long tongues,
— Their voices possessed of the brahmin sound,
— Their lion-like jaws,
— Their forty teeth, straight, white, and closely set,
— Their blue eyes,
— And their eyelashes like those of the king of the bulls.

[Having observed or heard of these marks of a buddha's body], they may then become delighted in mind and may think, "I, too, should strive to gain these physical marks and I, too, should strive to gain those dharmas gained by those who possess such physical marks." They may then straightaway generate the resolve to gain realization of *anuttara-samyak-saṃbodhi*.

Thus, it may be on account of any of these seven causes and conditions that one then generates the resolve to gain the realization of bodhi.

II. The Relative Probability of Success in These Seven Bases

Question: You have declared that there are these seven sorts of causes and conditions behind a person's generation of a bodhisattva's resolve. Is it the case that every one of these circumstances will result in success or is it rather the case that there will be success in some instances whereas, in other instances, there will be no success?

Response: It may not be the case that there will definitely be success resulting from all of these circumstances. It may be that there is success in some cases whereas no success results in other cases.

问曰。若尔者应解说。答
曰。

于七发心中。佛教令发心。
护法故发心。怜愍故发心。

如是三心者。必定得成就。
其馀四心者。不必皆成就。

[36a18]　　是七心中佛观其根
本。教令发心必得成。以不
空言故。若为尊重佛法为欲
守护。若于众生有大悲心。
如是三心必得成就。根本深
故。馀菩萨教令发心。见菩
萨所行发心。因大布施发
心。若见若闻佛相发心。是
四心多不成。或有成者。根
本微弱故[1]。

問曰。若爾者應解說。答
曰。

於七發心中。佛教令發心。
護法故發心。憐愍故發心。

如是三心者。必定得成就。
其餘四心者。不必皆成就。

[36a18]　　是七心中佛觀其根
本。教令發心必得成。以不
空言故。若為尊重佛法為欲
守護。若於眾生有大悲心。
如是三心必得成就。根本深
故。餘菩薩教令發心。見菩
薩所行發心。因大布施發
心。若見若聞佛相發心。是
四心多不成。或有成者。根
本微弱故[1]。

简体字　　　　　　　　　　　　正體字

Question: That being the case, one should proceed with an explanation of this matter.
Response:

Among the seven sorts of generation of resolve,
Where the Buddha has instructed one to generate resolve,
Where one generates resolve in order to protect the Dharma,
And where one generates resolve on account of pity,

Those possessed of the three motivations of this sort,
Will definitely be ones who find success in this.
As for the other four types of motivation,
It is not definite that they will be successful in every case.

Among these seven categories of resolve, where a buddha has contemplated the basis in one's faculties and then instructed one to generate the resolve, that will certainly result in success, this because [the Buddhas] do not utter words which are in vain.

So, too, in instances where [such resolve is generated] on account of revering and esteeming the Dharma of the Buddhas and being motivated by the will to protect it.

So, too, in those instances where one has brought forth the mind of great compassion for the sake of beings. These three categories of resolve will definitely result in success, this because the roots [of goodness] are deeply anchored.

In instances where other bodhisattvas have provided instruction which has influenced one to generate the resolve, in instances where one has observed the practices of bodhisattvas and thus generated the resolve, in instances where one has generated the resolve on account of an act of great giving, and in instances where one has generated the resolve on account of directly seeing or merely hearing about the physical marks [of a buddha]—most of these instances of generating the resolve do not result in success.

Still, it may indeed be that there will be success in these latter instances. [Failure to find success in such instances] is on account of the relative weakness of the roots [of goodness] which serve as their bases.

Chinese Text Variant Readings	Chinese Text Variant Readings
[35n03] 当=常 [宋] [元] [明] [宫]	[35n03] 當=常 [宋] [元] [明] [宫]
[35n04] 福=功 [宋] [元] [明] [宫]	[35n04] 福=功 [宋] [元] [明] [宫]
[35n05] 法忍=忍法 [宋] [元] [明] [宫]	[35n05] 法忍=忍法 [宋] [元] [明] [宫]
[36n01] 不分卷 [宋] [元] [明] [宫]	[36n01] 不分卷 [宋] [元] [明] [宫]

| 简体字 | 正體字 |

Part One Endnotes

1. This is Chapter Six from Ārya Nāgārjuna's *Ten Grounds Vibhāṣā* (*Daśabhūmika-vibhāṣā* / 十住毘婆沙論), drawn from the third fascicle of that work (T26.1521.35a-36a24).

2. This may well be a reference to the six perfections, the four immeasurable minds, and the three gates to liberation.

3. "Seventeen physical dharmas" is a speculative translation for *shen shiqi* (身十七). The text is ambiguous here. Digital scanning of the entire *Taisho* canon failed to turn up any plausible analogues of this list. It is possible this was once a standard list now found nowhere else in the extant Mahāyāna canon. Alternately, it may be that this phrase has been corrupted by an early scribal error.

4. As Nāgārjuna makes clear elsewhere, for one who aspires to course all the way along the Bodhisattva Path to ultimate realization of buddhahood, it is essential that they genuinely and solidly generate the resolve to gain the utmost, right, and perfect enlightenment *prior* to entering this "right and fixed position." This is why "unproduced-dharmas patience" is referenced here as having the potential to constituting a "downfall."

   We might justifiably wonder how such an otherwise exalted realization could be looked upon by the likes of Nāgārjuna with such implicit disapproval. It is because, absent genuine generation of highest-bodhi resolve, the diligent cultivator of good dharmas who gains such a realization will become irreversible on the path to arhatship, effective with realization of unproduced-dharmas patience, thus entirely eliminating the possibility of future buddhahood.

   Nāgārjuna even goes so far as to equate such a scenario with a tragedy far worse than falling into the hells, this because the hells, unlike being irreversibly destined toward arhatship, do not eliminate the possibility of future buddhahood. Notwithstanding the *Lotus Sutra* text (which apparent contradiction Nāgārjuna treats in his *Bodhisaṃbhāra-śāstra*), irreversibility on the arhatship path, with the exception of special cases such as those involving the *Lotus Sutra's* "closet bodhisattvas," entirely eliminates any future possibility of realizing buddhahood.

   This explanation is per Nāgārjuna's explanation in his *Bodhisaṃbhāra-śāstra* (菩提資糧論 – T32, no. 1660) which I have translated in its entirety (six fascicles, including its interwoven early Indian commentary). The translation is available from Kalavinka Press.

5. The "right and fixed position" referenced here is that of the bodhisattva who has by this point become invulnerable to being turned away from the path to buddhahood.

6.   "Vessantara" Pali reconstruction courtesy of Bhikkhu Bodhi who also suggests that the Sanskrit equivalent may be "Viśvantara."

Part Two:

EXHORTATION
to
RESOLVE ON BUDDHAHOOD

By the Dhyāna Master & Pureland Patriarch
Śramaṇa Sheng'an Shixian (1686–1734 CE)

Part Two Contents

EXHORTATION TO RESOLVE ON BUDDHAHOOD

新纂续藏经第六十二册 **No. 1179**
（省庵法师语录卷上。）

劝发菩提心文。

(X62n1179_p0234b17-237a06)

不肖愚下凡夫僧实贤。泣血稽颡。哀告现前大众。及当世净信男女等。唯愿慈悲。少加听察。尝闻入道要门。发心为首。修行急务。立愿居先。愿立则众生可度。心发则佛道堪成。苟不发广大心。立坚固愿。则纵经尘劫。依然还在轮回。虽有修行。总是徒劳辛苦。故华严经云。忘失菩提心。修诸善法。是名魔业。忘失尚尔。况未发乎。故知欲学如来乘。必先具发菩萨愿。不可缓也。然心愿差别。其相乃多。若不指陈。如何趣向。今为大众略而言之。相有其八。所谓邪正真伪大小偏圆是也。

新纂續藏經第六十二冊 **No. 1179**
（省庵法師語錄卷上。）

勸發菩提心文。

(X62n1179_p0234b17-237a06)

不肖愚下凡夫僧實賢。泣血稽顙。哀告現前大眾。及當世淨信男女等。唯願慈悲。少加聽察。嘗聞入道要門。發心為首。修行急務。立願居先。願立則眾生可度。心發則佛道堪成。苟不發廣大心。立堅固願。則縱經塵劫。依然還在輪回。雖有修行。總是徒勞辛苦。故華嚴經云。忘失菩提心。修諸善法。是名魔業。忘失尚爾。況未發乎。故知欲學如來乘。必先具發菩薩願。不可緩也。然心願差別。其相乃多。若不指陳。如何趣向。今為大眾略而言之。相有其八。所謂邪正真偽大小偏圓是也。

简体字　　　　　　　　　正體字

Exhortation to Resolve on Buddhahood

By Śramaṇa Sheng'an Shixian
of Hangzhou's Brahma Heaven Monastery

I. The Introductory Section
  A. First, The Mind's Vows as the Root of Cultivation.

This unworthy, foolish, and lowly common monk, Shixian, weeping tears of blood, bows down and makes this deeply felt proclamation to the present Great Assembly[1] as well as to the rest of this world's men and women of pure faith. I only pray that, extending kindness and compassion, they will briefly listen and reflect [upon this].

I have heard that among the essential gateway methods for entering the Path, generating the [bodhi] resolve is paramount. Among the critically urgent responsibilities involved in cultivation, the establishment of vows is foremost.

Once vows have been established, then beings may be brought across to liberation. When the resolution has been brought forth, then the path to buddhahood may be perfected. If one only fails to generate this expansively great resolve and establish solid vows, then, even if one courses on through kalpas as numerous as dust motes, one will still continue to abide in cyclic existence. Even though one may possess some achievement in cultivation, it is all only futilely-endured suffering.

Hence the *Floral Adornment Sutra* states: "If through forgetting it, one loses the bodhi resolve[2] while cultivating all manner of wholesome dharmas, these amount to demonic karmic actions."[3] If this is the case for merely "forgetting" it, how much the more would it be so where one has not yet even generated it. Thus, one should realize that if he aspires to study the vehicle of the Tathāgata,[4] it is essential to first become equipped with the generation of the bodhisattva vow.[5] This is not something which can be delayed.

  B. "Riddance" and "Implementation" in Generating Bodhi Resolve
    1. Bringing up the Categories and Enumerating Their Names

As for the distinctions involved in the mind's aspirations, their characteristic features are numerous. If one failed to point them out and explain them, how could one proceed to develop them? Now, for the sake of the Great Assembly, we shall speak of them in summary fashion. The characteristic features are eightfold, as follows: They are the so-called deviant or correct, genuine or false, great or small, and one-sided or perfect.

云何名为邪正真伪大小偏圆
邪。世有行人。一向修行。
不究自心。但知外务。或求
利养。或好名闻。或贪现世
欲乐。或望未来果报。如是
发心。名之为邪。既不求利
养名闻。又不贪欲乐果报。
唯为生死。为菩提。如是发
心。名之为正。念念上求佛
道。心心下化众生。闻佛道
长远。不生退怯。观众生难
度。不生厌倦。如登万仞之
山。必穷其顶。如上九层之
塔。必造其颠。如是发心。
名之为真。有罪不忏。有过
不除。内浊外清。始勤终
怠。虽有好心。多为名利之
所夹杂。虽有善法。复为罪
业之所染污。如是发心。名
之为伪。

云何名為邪正真偽大小偏圓
邪。世有行人。一向修行。
不究自心。但知外務。或求
利養。或好名聞。或貪現世
欲樂。或望未來果報。如是
發心。名之為邪。既不求利
養名聞。又不貪欲樂果報。
唯為生死。為菩提。如是發
心。名之為正。念念上求佛
道。心心下化眾生。聞佛道
長遠。不生退怯。觀眾生難
度。不生厭倦。如登萬仞之
山。必窮其頂。如上九層之
塔。必造其顛。如是發心。
名之為真。有罪不懺。有過
不除。內濁外清。始勤終
怠。雖有好心。多為名利之
所夾雜。雖有善法。復為罪
業之所染污。如是發心。名
之為偽。

簡体字   正體字

2. Distinguishing Their Characteristics Based on Their Names
a. Noting Their Names

What then does one mean by "deviant or correct, genuine or false, great or small, and one-sided or perfect"?

b. Distinguishing Their Characteristics

There exists in the world a class of practitioner pursuing cultivation with singular directness, but does not investigate his own mind and merely possesses an awareness of external matters. In some cases, he may seek for personal profit and offerings. In some cases, he may be fond of fame. In some cases, he may covet the desire-based pleasures of the present age. And in some cases, he may look with hopefulness to karmic rewards in the future. When one generates a resolve of this sort, this is what qualifies as "deviant."

It may be [on the other hand] that one does not seek for profit or fame and does not covet desire-based pleasures or karmic rewards. Rather one's efforts are solely for the sake of transcending cyclic birth-and-death[6] and realizing bodhi. When one generates a resolve of this sort, this is what qualifies as "correct."

As regards those above, one should seek in every mind-moment to search out the Path of the Buddha. As regards those below, one should strive in every thought to transform beings through teaching them. On hearing of the far-reaching and distant length of the Buddha Path, one should not retreat in timidity. On observing that beings are difficult to bring across to liberation, one should not allow oneself to become weary with disgust.

This is just as when one ascends a ten-thousand-meter mountain. One must be determined then to climb up to its very summit. And it is just as when one erects a nine-level stupa.[7] In doing so, one must certainly complete it through creating its crowning story. When one generates resolve of this sort, this is what qualifies as "genuine."

It may be that one has created karmic offenses and yet does not repent of them and it may be that one has committed transgressions and yet fails to do away with them. It may be that one is inwardly turbid while outwardly acting as if clear. It may be that one acts industriously at the beginning and yet becomes indolent in the end. It may be that, even though one possesses fine thoughts, they are for the most part admixed with concerns about reputation and wealth. And it may be that, even though one has taken up wholesome dharmas, one remains defiled by offense-laden karma. When one generates a resolve of this sort, this is what qualifies as "false."

众生界尽。我愿方尽。菩提
道成。我愿方成。如是发
心。名之为大。观三界如牢
狱。视生死如冤家。但期自
度。不欲度人。如是发心。
名之为小。若于心外见有众
生。及以佛道。愿度愿成。
功勋不忘。知见不泯。如是
发心。名之为偏。若知自性
是众生。故愿度脱。自性是
佛道。故愿成就。不见一法
离心别有。以虚空之心。发
虚空之愿。行虚空之行。证
虚空之果。亦无虚空之相可
得。如是发心。名之为圆。
知此八种差别。则知审察。
知审察。则知去取。知去
取。则可发心。云何审察。
谓我所发心。于此八中。为
邪为正。为真为伪。为大为
小。为偏为圆。

眾生界盡。我願方盡。菩提
道成。我願方成。如是發
心。名之為大。觀三界如牢
獄。視生死如冤家。但期自
度。不欲度人。如是發心。
名之為小。若於心外見有眾
生。及以佛道。願度願成。
功勳不忘。知見不泯。如是
發心。名之為偏。若知自性
是眾生。故願度脫。自性是
佛道。故願成就。不見一法
離心別有。以虛空之心。發
虛空之願。行虛空之行。證
虛空之果。亦無虛空之相可
得。如是發心。名之為圓。
知此八種差別。則知審察。
知審察。則知去取。知去
取。則可發心。云何審察。
謂我所發心。於此八中。為
邪為正。為真為偽。為大為
小。為偏為圓。

简体字

正體字

One resolves: "When the realm of sentient beings has come to an end, only then shall my vows come to an end. When the path to the realization of bodhi has become perfected, only then shall my vows be perfected." When one generates a resolve of this sort, this is what qualifies as "great."

It may be that one contemplates the three realms as like a prison, looks upon cyclic birth-and-death as like an enemy, aspires only to achieve one's own personal liberation, and does not desire to bring other people across to liberation. If one generates a resolve of this sort, this is what qualifies as "small."

It may be that one perceives that beings and the Buddha's Path exist outside of one's own mind and that, guided by this perception, one aspires to bring those beings across to liberation and perfect that path. In a circumstance of this sort, one remains unable to forget one's own meritorious service and remains unable to extinguish [attachment to] one's own knowledge and views. If one generates a resolve of this sort, this is what qualifies as "one-sided."

It may be that, realizing one's own nature is identical to that of beings, one aspires to bring them across to liberation. It may be that, realizing one's own nature corresponds to the Buddha Path, one consequently aspires to perfect it. [It may be that] one does not perceive even a single dharma existing apart from the mind. [And it may be that] one employs a mind cognizing emptiness to generate vows rooted in emptiness, to implement practices grounded in emptiness, and to realize the fruits of cognizing emptiness—all of this while remaining free of the view that there is any characteristic feature of emptiness which can be apprehended at all. If one generates a resolve of this sort, this is what qualifies as "perfect."

3. POINTING OUT AND DESCRIBING RIDDANCE AND IMPLEMENTATION

When one understands these eight types of distinctions, one then understands how to carry on "analytic reflection." When one understands how to carry on analytic reflection, one understands how to carry out "riddance and implementation." When one understands how to carry out riddance and implementation, one becomes able to [correctly] generate the [bodhi] resolve.

What is meant by "analytic reflection"? It refers to [an on-going analysis of and reflection upon] this resolve which we generate [whereby we recognize] whether it is deviant, whether it is correct, whether it is genuine, whether it is false, whether it is great, whether it is small, whether it is one-sided, or whether it is perfect.

云何去取。所谓去邪去伪。去小去偏。取正取真。取大取圆。如此发心。方得名为真正发菩提心也。此菩提心。诸善中王。必有因缘。方得发起。今言因缘。略有十种。何等为十。一者念佛重恩故。二者念父母恩故。三者念师长。恩故。四者念施主恩故。五者念众生恩故。六者念死生苦故。七者尊重己灵故。八者忏悔业障故。九者求生净土故。十者为念正法得久住故。云何念佛重恩。谓我释迦如来。最初发心。为我等故。行菩萨道。经无量劫。备受诸苦。

云何去取。所謂去邪去偽。去小去偏。取正取真。取大取圓。如此發心。方得名為真正發菩提心也。此菩提心。諸善中王。必有因緣。方得發起。今言因緣。略有十種。何等為十。一者念佛重恩故。二者念父母恩故。三者念師長。恩故。四者念施主恩故。五者念眾生恩故。六者念死生苦故。七者尊重己靈故。八者懺悔業障故。九者求生淨土故。十者為念正法得久住故。云何念佛重恩。謂我釋迦如來。最初發心。為我等故。行菩薩道。經無量劫。備受諸苦。

简体字   正體字

What is meant by "riddance and implementation"? It refers to ridding oneself of the deviant, ridding oneself of the false, ridding oneself of the small, and ridding oneself of the one-sided while simultaneously implementing the correct, implementing the genuine, implementing the great, and implementing the perfect.

When one generates a resolve of this sort, one then succeeds in carrying forth with what qualifies as the genuine and correct generation of the bodhi resolve.

II. The Doctrinal Section Proper

  A. Praising Qualities and Explaining Causal Bases

This bodhi resolve is the king among all forms of goodness. It is certainly the case that there are causal bases upon which one then becomes able to generate it.

  B. Noting the Number and Listing the Names

Now, when we speak of causal bases, generally speaking, there are ten categories.

Of what do these ten consist?

The first is mindfulness of the extreme kindness of the Buddha.

The second is mindfulness of the kindness of one's parents.

The third is mindfulness of the kindness of teachers and seniors.

The fourth is mindfulness of the kindness of benefactors.

The fifth is mindfulness of the kindness of beings.

The sixth is mindfulness of the sufferings in cyclic birth-and-death.

The seventh is reverence for one's own spiritual mind.

The eighth is repentance of one's karmic obstacles.

The ninth is the aspiration to gain rebirth in the Pureland.

The tenth is mindful concern that right Dharma long endure.

  C. Next, Substantiation of the Bases

    1. Mindfulness of the Extreme Kindness of the Buddha

What is intended by "mindfulness of the extreme kindness of the Buddha"? This is in reference to when our Shākyamuni Tathāgata himself initially generated the [bodhi] resolve. It was for our sakes that he coursed in the Bodhisattva Path, passing through a countless number of kalpas undergoing in full measure every sort of suffering.

我造业时。佛则哀怜。方便教化。而我愚痴。不知信受。我堕地狱。佛复悲痛。欲代我苦。而我业重。不能救拔。我生人道。佛以方便。令种善根。世世生生。随逐于我。心无暂舍。佛初出世。我尚沉沦。今得人身。佛已灭度。何罪而生末法。何福而预出家。何障而不见金身。何幸而躬逢舍利。如是思惟。向使不种善根。何以得闻佛法。不闻佛法。焉知常受佛恩。此恩此德。邱山难喻。自非发广大心。行菩萨道。建立佛法。救度众生。纵使粉骨碎身。岂能酬答。是为发菩提心第一因缘也。云何念父母恩。哀哀父母。生我劬劳。十月三年。怀胎乳哺。推乾去湿。嚼苦

我造業時。佛則哀憐。方便教化。而我愚癡。不知信受。我墮地獄。佛復悲痛。欲代我苦。而我業重。不能救拔。我生人道。佛以方便。令種善根。世世生生。隨逐於我。心無暫捨。佛初出世。我尚沉淪。今得人身。佛已滅度。何罪而生末法。何福而預出家。何障而不見金身。何幸而躬逢舍利。如是思惟。向使不種善根。何以得聞佛法。不聞佛法。焉知常受佛恩。此恩此德。邱山難喻。自非發廣大心。行菩薩道。建立佛法。救度眾生。縱使粉骨碎身。豈能酬答。是為發菩提心第一因緣也。云何念父母恩。哀哀父母。生我劬勞。十月三年。懷胎乳哺。推乾去濕。嚼苦

简体字   正體字

Whenever we have created karma, the Buddha has felt anguished pity for us and set forth skillful expedients to teach us. Even so, we have been so foolish that we have failed to realize that we should have faith in and accept such teaching.

Whenever we have fallen into the hells, the Buddha again ached with compassion and wished to take on such sufferings for us. However, our karma has been so heavy that he was unable to rescue and extricate us from such difficulties.

When we regained rebirth in the human realm, the Buddha employed skillful means to influence us to plant roots of goodness and then, in life-after-life, followed along after us, his mindfulness never abandoning us for even a moment.

When the Buddha first came into the world, we were still sunken in misery. Now that we have regained the human body, the Buddha has already passed into cessation. What karmic transgressions have we committed to be born in the Dharma-ending age? What merit have we created to be able to leave the home life? What karmic obstacles have we generated to be unable to personally view his golden body? What good fortune indeed that we now personally encounter his *śarīra*.[8]

And so one reflects in this fashion: "Had we failed to plant roots of goodness, how could we have succeeded in hearing the Dharma of the Buddha? Had we not heard the Dharma of the Buddha, how could we even be aware of constantly receiving these kindnesses of the Buddha?"

These kindnesses and these meritorious qualities are difficult to describe even by comparing them to a mountain. If we were to fail to generate the vast and magnificent resolve, course in the Bodhisattva Path, establish the Dharma of the Buddha, and rescue beings by bringing them across to liberation, then, even were we to crush our own body and splinter our own bones, how could we be able to repay this?

This is the first of the causal bases for generation of the bodhi resolve.

2. Mindfulness of the Kindness of One's Parents

What then is intended by "mindfulness of the kindness of one's parents"? One reflects, "What heartache I feel recalling the intense labors of my parents in giving birth to me—for ten months and three years, carrying me in the womb and nursing me, 'placing me into the dry and getting rid of the wet,'[9] 'swallowing the bitter and

吐甘。才得成人。指望绍继门风。供承祭祀。今我等既已出家。滥称释子。忝号沙门。甘旨不供。祭埽不给。生不能养其口体。死不能导其神灵。于世间则为大损。于出世又无实益。两途既失。重罪难逃。如是思惟。唯有百劫千生。常行佛道。十方三世。普度众生。则不唯一生父母。生生父母俱蒙拔济。不唯一人父母。人人父母尽可超升。是为发菩提心第二因缘也。云何念师长恩。父母虽能生育我身。若无世间师长。则不知礼义。若无出世师长。则不解佛法。不知礼义。则同于异类。不解佛法。则何异俗人。今我等粗知礼义。略

吐甘。才得成人。指望紹繼門風。供承祭祀。今我等既已出家。濫稱釋子。忝號沙門。甘旨不供。祭埽不給。生不能養其口體。死不能導其神靈。於世間則為大損。於出世又無實益。兩途既失。重罪難逃。如是思惟。唯有百劫千生。常行佛道。十方三世。普度眾生。則不唯一生父母。生生父母俱蒙拔濟。不唯一人父母。人人父母盡可超昇。是為發菩提心第二因緣也。云何念師長恩。父母雖能生育我身。若無世間師長。則不知禮義。若無出世師長。則不解佛法。不知禮義。則同於異類。不解佛法。則何異俗人。今我等粗知禮義。略

简体字　　　　　　　　　　　正體字

giving up the sweet,' so that I then succeeded in becoming a man. They pointed out to me with hopefulness how I might carry on the family's good name and the tradition of making offerings and paying reverence to its spirits."

Now, since we have already left the home life, we are, through exaggeration, called "Sons of the Buddha" and are, although unworthy of the name, referred to as "*śramaṇas*."[10] It is on this account that we do not carry out the offerings of delicacies to [the family spirits] and do not lend any assistance by paying reverence or sweeping at their grave sites. While they are still alive, we are unable to provide for their nourishment. Once they have died, we are unable to guide forth their spirits. Thus, as regards the world, we greatly diminish its resources. As regards that which lies beyond the world, we provide no genuine benefit there, either. If thus we are failures with respect to both of these paths, then such heavy karmic offenses would be difficult to escape.

When we reflect in this manner, [we see that] it is only through constantly coursing in the Buddha's Path throughout thousands of births across hundreds of kalpas spanning the ten directions and the three periods of time that we will be able to universally bring beings across to liberation. If we do this, then it will not be solely one's own father and mother from a single lifetime [who shall benefit]. Rather, one's fathers and mothers from life-after-life shall all be the recipients of extrication and rescue. And it shall not be but a single person's fathers and mothers, but rather the fathers and mothers of everyone who will all be able to leap over [the abyss] and ascend. This is the second of the causal bases for generation of the bodhi resolve.

3. Mindfulness of the Kindness of Teachers and Seniors

What then is intended by "mindfulness of the kindness of teachers and seniors"? One reflects, "Although my father and mother were able to give birth to and raise up my physical body, still, if it were not for my worldly teachers and seniors, I would not understand propriety or righteousness. If it were not for my transcendental teachers and seniors, I would not understand the Dharma of the Buddha. If I failed to have an awareness of ceremonial propriety and righteousness, then I would be identical to other classes of beings.[11] If I failed to understand the Dharma of the Buddha, then what distinction would there be between me and the common person?"

The fact that we now possess a rather coarse awareness of

解佛法袈裟被体。戒品沾
身。此之重恩。从师长得。
若求小果。仅能自利。今为
大乘。普愿利人。则世出世
间二种师长。俱蒙利益。是
为发菩提心第三因缘也。云
何念施主恩。谓我等今者日
用所资。并非己有。三时粥
饭。四季衣裳。疾病所须。
身口所费。此皆出自他力。
将为我用。彼则竭力躬耕。
尚难餬口。我则安坐受食。
犹不称心。彼则纺织不已。
犹自艰难。我于安服有馀。
宁知爱惜。彼则荜门蓬户。
扰攘终身。我则广宇闲庭。
优悠卒岁。以彼劳而供我
逸。于心安乎。将他利而润
己身。于理顺乎。自非悲智
双运。福慧二严。檀信沾
恩。

解佛法袈裟被體。戒品沾
身。此之重恩。從師長得。
若求小果。僅能自利。今為
大乘。普願利人。則世出世
間二種師長。俱蒙利益。是
為發菩提心第三因緣也。云
何念施主恩。謂我等今者日
用所資。並非己有。三時粥
飯。四季衣裳。疾病所須。
身口所費。此皆出自他力。
將為我用。彼則竭力躬耕。
尚難餬口。我則安坐受食。
猶不稱心。彼則紡織不已。
猶自艱難。我於安服有餘。
寧知愛惜。彼則蓽門蓬戶。
擾攘終身。我則廣宇閒庭。
優悠卒歲。以彼勞而供我
逸。於心安乎。將他利而潤
己身。於理順乎。自非悲智
雙運。福慧二嚴。檀信沾
恩。

简体字   正體字

ceremonial propriety and righteousness and now possess a general understanding of the Buddha's Dharma, wear the *kāṣāya* robe[12] and are personally imbued with the codes of moral restraint—these emblems of extremely weighty kindnesses were all gained from our teachers and seniors. If we were now to strive for the achievement of lesser sorts of fruits of the Path,[13] we would only be able to accomplish our own self benefit. But if we now, for the sake of the priorities of the Great Vehicle, make a universal vow to benefit others, then the two classes of teachers and seniors—both the worldly and the transcendental—will all receive benefits from this. This is the third of the causal bases for generation of the bodhi resolve.

4. Mindfulness of the Kindness of Benefactors

What then is intended by "mindfulness of the kindness of benefactors"? One reflects, "That which I rely on for daily use is certainly not something which comes from me. The two mealtimes of gruel and of rice, the clothing appropriate to the four seasons, the necessities for treating illness—everything used by the body or consumed as sustenance—these are all produced through the work of others and then brought forth for me to use.

"As for those benefactors, they must exhaust their strength in personally cultivating the fields and even then find it difficult to make a living to feed the family. As for me, I sit here in peace and receive food from others, perhaps even then not finding it agreeable.

"As for those benefactors, though they may be ceaselessly busy at sewing [for others], they may still be in difficult straits themselves. As for me, I am well-clothed and even have more than I need. I should know to be sparing [in the use of donations].

"As for those benefactors, they live where 'the gates are made of rushes and the windows are made of grass,'[14] enduring disturbances and troubles for their entire lives. As for myself, I abide in vast halls and vacant courtyards, wandering in leisure to the very end of each year. For me to take the fruits of their labors as a contribution to my own reclusive life—is this a matter which makes the mind feel at ease? For me to take the benefits which they have earned as the basis for my own personal convenience—is this a circumstance which accords with principle?

"Were I to fail to carry forth the simultaneous exercise of compassion and wisdom while also accumulating the two 'adornments' of merit and wisdom[15]—if the *dāna*-providing[16] faithful thus remained unable to absorb [the benefits from their] kindnesses and

众生受赐。则粒米寸丝。酬偿有分。恶报难逃。是为发菩提心第四因缘也。云何念众生恩。谓我与众生。从旷劫来。世世生生。互为父母。彼此有恩。今虽隔世昏迷。互不相识。以理推之。岂无报效。今之披毛带角。安知非昔为其子乎。今之蠕动蜎飞。安知不曾为我父乎。每见幼离父母。长而容貌都忘。何况宿世亲缘。今则张王难记。彼其号呼于地狱之下。宛转于饿鬼之中。苦痛谁知。饥虚安诉。我虽不见不闻。彼必求拯求济。非经不能陈此事。非佛不能道此言。彼邪见人。何足以知此。是故菩萨观于蝼蚁。皆是过去父母。未来诸佛。常思利益。念报其恩。是为发菩提心第五因缘也。

眾生受賜。則粒米寸絲。酬償有分。惡報難逃。是為發菩提心第四因緣也。云何念眾生恩。謂我與眾生。從曠劫來。世世生生。互為父母。彼此有恩。今雖隔世昏迷。互不相識。以理推之。豈無報效。今之披毛帶角。安知非昔為其子乎。今之蠕動蜎飛。安知不曾為我父乎。每見幼離父母。長而容貌都忘。何況宿世親緣。今則張王難記。彼其號呼於地獄之下。宛轉於餓鬼之中。苦痛誰知。飢虛安訴。我雖不見不聞。彼必求拯求濟。非經不能陳此事。非佛不能道此言。彼邪見人。何足以知此。是故菩薩觀於螻蟻。皆是過去父母。未來諸佛。常思利益。念報其恩。是為發菩提心第五因緣也。

简体字　　　　　　　　　正體字

beings thus could not receive [appropriate reward for their] generosity—then there would be a measure of repayment of indebtedness remaining due even on each grain of rice and on each inch of thread [which I've been given]. As a result, the retribution for evil deeds will become a difficult consequence to escape." This is the fourth of the causal bases for generation of the bodhi resolve.

5. Mindfulness of the Kindness of Beings

What then is intended by "mindfulness of the kindness of beings"? One reflects, "From far off kalpas ago on forward to the present, other beings and I have served each other as fathers and mothers in lifetime after lifetime." In this there have been kindnesses they have proffered to us. Although now separated from those lives and hence so confused that we do not recognize each other, when we reflect on this principle, how can we fail to reciprocate?

How can one know that those beings who now wear fur and carry horns are not one's children from the past? How can one know that those who are now but wriggling worms, larvae, and flying insects were not previously my father? It is commonly seen that, for those who separate from their parents when still young, once grown, they forget their faces entirely. How much the more so would this be the case for those with whom I possess that condition of their having being a previous-life relative. This being the case, then it is difficult to remember whether they were named "Zhang" or named "Wang."

As for those [relatives], who [among us] would be aware of their screams down in the hells or their turning about in the realm of the hungry ghosts, undergoing such suffering and pain? As for their hunger and desolation—how would they be able to present an appeal [to us]? Although I do not now see or hear them, they are certainly longing to be saved and seeking to be rescued.

Were it not for the Sutras, one would be unable to reveal this state of affairs. Were it not for the Buddha, one would be unable to utter this description. Those others, possessed as they are of erroneous views—how could they be qualified to even know of this? Thus it is that, when a bodhisattva observes crickets and ants, he realizes that each of them was his father or his mother sometime in the past. He realizes that each of them shall become buddhas in the future. He constantly ponders how to benefit them and he continues to bear in mind the responsibility of repaying their kindnesses. This is the fifth of the causal bases for generation of the bodhi resolve.

云何念生死苦。谓我与众生
从旷劫来。常在生死。未得
解脱。人间天上。此界他
方。出没万端升。沈片刻。
俄焉而天。俄焉而人。俄焉
而地狱畜生饿鬼。黑门朝出
而暮还。铑窟暂离而又入。
登刀山也。则举体无完肤。
攀剑树也。则方寸皆割裂。
热铑不除饥。吞之则肝肠尽
烂。洋铜难疗渴。饮之则骨
肉都糜。利锯解之。则断而
复续。巧风吹之。则死已还
生。猛火城中。忍听叫嚣之
惨。煎熬盘里。但闻苦痛之
声。冰冻始凝。则状似青莲
蕊结。血肉既裂则身如红藕
华开。一夜死生。地下每经
万遍。一朝苦痛。人间已过
百年。频烦狱卒疲劳。谁信

云何念生死苦。謂我與眾生
從曠劫來。常在生死。未得
解脫。人間天上。此界他
方。出沒萬端昇。沈片刻。
俄焉而天。俄焉而人。俄焉
而地獄畜生餓鬼。黑門朝出
而暮還。鋑窟暫離而又入。
登刀山也。則舉體無完膚。
攀劍樹也。則方寸皆割裂。
熱鋑不除飢。吞之則肝腸盡
爛。洋銅難療渴。飲之則骨
肉都糜。利鋸解之。則斷而
復續。巧風吹之。則死已還
生。猛火城中。忍聽叫嘮之
慘。煎熬盤裏。但聞苦痛之
聲。冰凍始凝。則狀似青蓮
蕊結。血肉既裂則身如紅藕
華開。一夜死生。地下每經
萬遍。一朝苦痛。人間已過
百年。頻煩獄卒疲勞。誰信

简体字   正體字

6.　Mindfulness of the Sufferings of Cyclic Birth and Death

What then is intended by "mindfulness of the sufferings of cyclic birth and death"? One reflects, "From far off kalpas ago on forward to the present, I and other beings have constantly dwelt in cyclic birth-and-death and, even now have not yet succeeded in gaining liberation. Whether it has been among humans, up in the heavens, here in this realm, or off in other regions, our emerging and sinking away has been in a myriad different forms."

This ascending and submerging occurs so suddenly that, one moment we are in the heavens and then, in a trice, we are back among humans. From there, in a mere instant, we may fall back down into the hells, among animals, or into the midst of the hungry ghosts.

One may go forth from the black gates of hell in the morning and then return again in the evening. One may depart from the iron cave temporarily, but then return and enter it yet again.

When one climbs the mountain of knives, there remains no place on the body where the skin remains intact. When one climbs the tree of swords, then every inch of the body becomes sliced open. Hot iron does not get rid of hunger. When one swallows it, the liver and intestines are all scorched into ruination. It is hard for molten copper to cure a person's thirst. When one drinks it down, the bones and flesh are all burned into a paste.

When sharp saws slice open the body, though cut apart, it joins itself back together. Then an artful wind arises which blows upon it and causes it, though already dead, to come back to life.[17]

In the "city of fierce fire," one must bear listening to the pitiful misery of screaming and howling. Where [hell-dwellers] are being stewed in a cauldron, one hears only the sounds of intense agony. When, [in the cold hells], the icy cold first starts to harden [the body into ice], its form becomes similar to the closed bud of a blue lotus. Once the blood vessels and flesh have been split open [by expansion of the ice], the body then resembles the fully-blossomed red lotus.

In just a single [human-realm] night, one goes through death and rebirth in the hells ten thousand times. In just a single [human-realm] morning, one passes through what would be like a hundred years of intense agony among humans.

Thus one repeatedly troubles the guardians of the hells, driving them to the point of exhaustion. But who now actually believes in

阎翁教诫。受时知苦虽悔恨以何追脱已还忘。其作业也如故。鞭驴出血。谁知吾母之悲。牵豕就屠。焉识乃翁之痛。食其子而不知。文王尚尔。啖其亲而未识。凡类皆然。当年恩爱。今作冤家。昔日寇雠。今成骨肉。昔为母而今为妇。旧是翁而新作夫。宿命知之。则可羞可耻。天眼视之。则可笑可怜。粪秽丛中。十月包藏难过。脓血道里。一时倒下可怜。少也何知。东西莫辨。长而有识。贪欲便生。须臾而老病相寻。迅速而无常又至。风火交煎。神识于中溃乱。精血既竭。皮肉自外干枯。无一毛而不被针钻。有一窍而皆从刀割。龟之将烹。其脱壳也犹

閻翁教誡。受時知苦雖悔恨以何追脫已還忘。其作業也如故。鞭驢出血。誰知吾母之悲。牽豕就屠。焉識乃翁之痛。食其子而不知。文王尚爾。啖其親而未識。凡類皆然。當年恩愛。今作冤家。昔日寇讎。今成骨肉。昔為母而今為婦。舊是翁而新作夫。宿命知之。則可羞可恥。天眼視之。則可笑可憐。糞穢叢中。十月包藏難過。膿血道裏。一時倒下可憐。少也何知。東西莫辨。長而有識。貪欲便生。須臾而老病相尋。迅速而無常又至。風火交煎。神識於中潰亂。精血既竭。皮肉自外乾枯。無一毛而不被針鑽。有一竅而皆從刀割。龜之將烹。其脫殼也猶

简体字　　　　　　　　正體字

the remonstrances of old Yama?[18] When forced to undergo [such punishments], one realizes the sufferings [following on bad actions]. Even though one then feels deep regret over one's transgressions, how could one go back at that point [and undo them]? Later, once set free [from the hells], one forgets yet again. Then, in one's karmic actions, one behaves just the same way as one did in the past.

When one whips the donkey to the point of drawing blood, who could know, "This is the anguish of my own mother"?[19] When one leads away the hog to be butchered, how could one recognize that its pain is that of one's very own elderly father?[20]

One could be eating the flesh of one's own son and yet fail to realize it. If this was the case even for King Wen who [was tricked into] consuming the flesh of his own relatives, then this would be true for any common person.[21]

Those who in years past related to us with kindness and affection may now be acting as our rivals. Those who in earlier days were enemies may now be seen as our very "flesh-and-blood."[22] One's past-life mother may be the present life's wife. It may be that he who long ago was a father has now recently become one's husband. When someone possessing knowledge of past lives becomes aware of this, he may find it a basis for chagrin and embarrassment. When one observes it with the heavenly eye, one may find it laughable and pathetic.

One endures the difficulty of ten months in the womb amidst fecal impurities and, passing through the canal of viscous fluids and blood, suddenly turns upside-down and descends in a pitiful state.[23]

When one is still young, what does one know? One cannot even distinguish east from west. As one grows up and one's consciousness develops, desires then develop. In but a short time, aging and sickness both chase along behind.

Then, so swiftly, impermanence arrives yet again. One is roasted in a convergence of elemental wind and fire. One's spirit and consciousness disperse and become muddled. Once one's yin-essence and blood have become exhausted, one's skin and flesh dry and wither from without. There is not a single hair-pore which does not feel as if reamed by needles. Wherever there is an opening in the body, one feels as if is stabbed by a knife.

When one is preparing a tortoise for stewing, [the agony it endures] in having its shell ripped off [may be said to be] relatively

易。神之欲謝。其去体也倍
难。心无常主。类商贾而处
处奔驰。身无定形。似房屋
而频频迁徙。大千尘点难穷
往返之身。四海波涛。孰计
别离之泪。峨峨积骨。过彼
崇山。莽莽横尸。多于大
地。向使不闻佛语。此事谁
见谁闻。未睹佛经。此理焉
知焉觉。其或依前贪恋。仍
旧痴迷。祇恐万劫千生。一
错百错。人身难得而易失
良。时易往而难追。道路冥
冥。别离长久。三途恶报。
还自受之。痛不可言。谁当
相代。兴言及此。能不寒
心。是故宜应断生死流。出
爱欲海。自他兼济。彼岸同
登。旷劫殊勋。

易。神之欲謝。其去體也倍
難。心無常主。類商賈而處
處奔馳。身無定形。似房屋
而頻頻遷徙。大千塵點難窮
往返之身。四海波濤。孰計
別離之淚。峨峨積骨。過彼
崇山。莽莽横尸。多於大
地。向使不聞佛語。此事誰
見誰聞。未睹佛經。此理焉
知焉覺。其或依前貪戀。仍
舊癡迷。祇恐萬劫千生。一
錯百錯。人身難得而易失
良。時易往而難追。道路冥
冥。別離長久。三途惡報。
還自受之。痛不可言。誰當
相代。興言及此。能不寒
心。是故宜應斷生死流。出
愛欲海。自他兼濟。彼岸同
登。曠劫殊勳。

简体字   正體字

easeful [when compared to the discomforts of death]. When one's spirit is about to retreat, its discarding of the body is doubly difficult to endure.

The mind has no enduring power to control the course of things. It is analogous to a traveling merchant who is forever running off from one place to the next. The bodies which one inhabits have no fixed form. In this they are comparable to houses from which one is forced to move time and time again. Just as with the dust motes of a great chiliocosm[24]—it is difficult indeed to trace back all of one's physical comings and goings.

Even were one to take the billowing waves of the four great oceans as a comparison, how could one measure all of the tears which have streamed down because of forced separation [from one's loved ones]? The towering heap of one's past-life skeletons would rise above even those highest of mountains. The immense accumulation of one's fallen corpses would be more massive than this entire great earth.

Were it not for hearing the words of the Buddha, who would be able to perceive this matter and who would be able even to hear of it? If one had not already laid eyes on the scriptures of the Buddha, how could one become aware of this principle and how could one awaken [to its reality]?

One might otherwise simply fall into relying on one's former affections and, as always in the past, continue on in delusion and confusion. One could only fear then that, in the thousands of lives across a myriad kalpas, a single error would become a hundred errors. The human body is a difficult thing to gain, but easy indeed to lose. The good times pass by so easily and then become difficult to retrieve.

The road ahead is dark and obscure. Once one becomes separated [from the human body], it shall be for a long, long time. The horrible retributions of the three wretched destinies[25] come back around and one is bound to undergo them oneself. The agony is indescribable. Who would stand in for us then?

Now that this flourish of words has reached this point, how could one fail to feel one's heart grow cold? Thus it is now only appropriate that one cut short the stream of cyclic births and deaths, extricate oneself from the ocean of desire, rescue both one's self and others, and climb together onto the other shore. The most excellent form of meritorious service which one might perform in a vast

在此一举。是为发菩提心第六因缘也。云何尊重己灵谓我现前一心。直下与释迦如来无二无别。云何世尊无量劫来。早成正觉而我等昏迷颠倒。尚做凡夫。又佛世尊则具有无量神通智慧。功德庄严。而我等则但有无量业系烦恼生死缠缚。心性是一。迷悟天渊。静言思之。岂不可耻。譬如无价宝珠。没在淤泥。视同瓦砾。不加爱重。是故宜应以无量善法。对治烦恼。修德有功。则性德方显。如珠被濯。悬在高幢。洞达光明。映蔽一切。可谓不孤佛化。不负己灵。是为发菩提心第七因缘也。云何忏悔业障。经言犯一吉罗。如四天王寿五百岁。堕泥犁中。吉罗小罪尚获此报。何况

在此一舉。是為發菩提心第六因緣也。云何尊重己靈謂我現前一心。直下與釋迦如來無二無別。云何世尊無量劫來。早成正覺而我等昏迷顛倒。尚做凡夫。又佛世尊則具有無量神通智慧。功德莊嚴。而我等則但有無量業繫煩惱生死纏縛。心性是一。迷悟天淵。靜言思之。豈不可恥。譬如無價寶珠。沒在淤泥。視同瓦礫。不加愛重。是故宜應以無量善法。對治煩惱。修德有功。則性德方顯。如珠被濯。懸在高幢。洞達光明。映蔽一切。可謂不孤佛化。不負己靈。是為發菩提心第七因緣也。云何懺悔業障。經言犯一吉羅。如四天王壽五百歲。墮泥犁中。吉羅小罪尚獲此報。何況

简体字   正體字

stretch of kalpas is accomplished by doing this one single deed. This is the sixth of the causal bases for generation of the bodhi resolve.

7. Reverence for One's Own Spiritual Mind

What is meant by "reverence for one's own spiritual mind"? One reflects, "This presently manifest one mind of mine as it is right now—comparing it to that of Shākyamuni Tathāgata—they are not two separate entities. They have nothing distinguishing them.

Why then is it that, early on, the Bhagavān[26] already realized the right enlightenment countless kalpas ago whereas we are still confused, are still ruled by inverted views, and are still but fool-ish common people? Additionally, as for the Buddha, the Bhagavān, he embodies countless sorts of spiritual superknowledges and wis-dom while also being adorned with all of the meritorious qualities. We, on the other hand, possess only countless varieties of karmic fetters and afflictions and remain wholly tied down in the sphere of cyclic births and deaths.

The nature of the mind in these two cases is singular. Nonetheless, the difference between confusion and awakening is as vast as the gulf between the heavens and the earth. When one quietly contem-plates this, how could one *not* feel ashamed?

[This spiritual mind] is like a priceless jewel which has become sunken in the mud and which thus is looked upon just like broken tiles or rubble. We devote no caring concern to it at all.

Hence it is only right that we should take up the countless sorts of good dharmas to counter the afflictions. As the meritorious qual-ity of cultivation produces results, the meritorious quality of one's nature will then become manifest. This is comparable to subject-ing that jewel to cleaning and then suspending it aloft in a canopy where its penetrating brilliance shines everywhere. This then may be said to qualify as not failing in gratitude for the teaching of the Buddha and not turning one's back on one's own spiritual mind. This is the seventh of the causal bases for generation of the bodhi resolve.

8. Repentance of One's Karmic Obstacles

What then is intended by "repentance of one's karmic obstacles"? A sutra states that if one merely transgresses a single *duṣkṛta* precept,[27] one will fall into *niraya*[28] for a period of time equaling five-hundred years in the heavens of the Four Heavenly Kings.[29] If one might undergo such severe retribution for transgressing a minor *duṣkṛta* precept, how much the more might this be the case for committing

重罪。其报难言。今我等日
用之中。一举一动。恒违戒
律。一［歹＊食］一水。频犯
尸罗。一日所犯。亦应无
量。何况终身历劫。所起之
罪。更不可言矣。且以五戒
言之。十人九犯。少露多
藏。五戒名为优婆塞戒。尚
不具足。何况沙弥比丘菩萨
等戒。又不必言矣。问其
名。则曰我比丘也。问其
实。则尚不足为优婆塞也。
岂不可愧哉。当知佛戒不受
则已。受则不可毁犯。不犯
则已。犯则终必堕落。若非
自慠慠他。自伤伤他。身口
并切。声泪俱下。普与众
生。求哀忏悔。则千生万
劫。恶报难逃。是为发菩提
心第八因缘也。云何求生净
土。谓在此土修行。其进道
也难。彼土往生。其成佛
也。易。易故

重罪。其報難言。今我等日
用之中。一舉一動。恒違戒
律。一［歹＊食］一水。頻犯
尸羅。一日所犯。亦應無
量。何況終身歷劫。所起之
罪。更不可言矣。且以五戒
言之。十人九犯。少露多
藏。五戒名為優婆塞戒。尚
不具足。何況沙彌比丘菩薩
等戒。又不必言矣。問其
名。則曰我比丘也。問其
實。則尚不足為優婆塞也。
豈不可愧哉。當知佛戒不受
則已。受則不可毀犯。不犯
則已。犯則終必墮落。若非
自慠慠他。自傷傷他。身口
併切。聲淚俱下。普與眾
生。求哀懺悔。則千生萬
劫。惡報難逃。是為發菩提
心第八因緣也。云何求生淨
土。謂在此土修行。其進道
也難。彼土往生。其成佛
也。易。易故

简体字

正體字

a major transgression? The retribution involved would be difficult even to describe.

Now, in the course of our daily lives, in every gesture and every movement, we are continually transgressing the moral precept codes. With every meal and every drink of water, we go against *śīla*[30] multiple times. Thus the transgressions committed in a single day would be countless. How much the more so would this be the case for this entire life and throughout the time we have coursed through the kalpas. Then, the karmic offenses generated would be even more impossible to describe.

Additionally, just to discuss this with regard to the five precepts, nine of every ten persons might be said to have transgressed against them. These transgressions are seldom revealed and are usually concealed. Now, the five precepts are referred to as the *upāsaka's* lay precepts.[31] If one is unable to fulfill even those requirements, how much the more would this be the case for the *śrāmaṇera*,[32] bhikshu,[33] and bodhisattva precepts. For those, it would be even less necessary to describe [the seriousness of] the situation.

When one is asked one's name, one replies, "I am a *bhikshu...*," however, were one to inquire into the reality of the matter, then one might not even be qualified to be an *upāsaka*. How could this not be cause for feeling ashamed?

One should realize that failing to take the precepts of the Buddha is one thing. But, once one has taken them, one must not transgress them. Refraining from transgressing them is one thing. But if one actually does go ahead and transgressed against them, then in the end, one will certainly fall.

If one fails to take pity on oneself and take pity on others, if one fails to feel regret for oneself while also feeling regret for [one's transgressions against] others, if one fails, with body and voice intently joined in crying aloud and shedding tears while seeking in anguish to repent before all beings, then the horrible retributions earned in thousands of lifetimes across myriads of kalpas will be difficult to escape. This is the eighth of the causal bases for generation of the bodhi resolve.

9. The Aspiration to Gain Rebirth in the Pureland

What then is intended by "the aspiration to gain rebirth in the Pureland"?[34] This refers to the fact that advancing on the Path when cultivating in this land is difficult whereas it is easy to achieve buddhahood once one has taken rebirth in that land. Because it is easy,

一生可致。难故累劫未成。
是以往圣前贤。人人趣向。
千经万论。处处指归。末世
修行。无越于此。然经称少
善不生。多福乃致。言多
福。则莫若执持名号。言多
善。则莫若发广大心。是以
暂持圣号。胜于布施百年。
一发大心。超过修行历劫。
盖念佛本期作佛。大心不
发。则虽念奚为。发心原为
修行。净土不生。则虽发易
退。是则下菩提种。耕以念
佛之犁。道果自然增长。乘
大愿船。入于净土之海。西
方决定往生。是为发菩提心
第九因缘也。云何令正法久
住。谓我世尊无量劫来。

一生可致。難故累劫未成。
是以往聖前賢。人人趣向。
千經萬論。處處指歸。末世
修行。無越於此。然經稱少
善不生。多福乃致。言多
福。則莫若執持名號。言多
善。則莫若發廣大心。是以
暫持聖號。勝於布施百年。
一發大心。超過修行歷劫。
蓋念佛本期作佛。大心不
發。則雖念奚為。發心原為
修行。淨土不生。則雖發易
退。是則下菩提種。耕以念
佛之犁。道果自然增長。乘
大願船。入於淨土之海。西
方決定往生。是為發菩提心
第九因緣也。云何令正法久
住。謂我世尊無量劫來。

简体字

正體字

one may reach the goal in a single lifetime when there, whereas, because of the difficulties, one may not have reached it even after a series of kalpas when here.

It is on account of this that the āryas[35] of the past and the worthies who were here before us all finaly directed themselves thither. In a thousand scriptures and in a myriad treatises, in place after place, one is directed to return there. As for cultivating a practice in the Dharma-ending age, there are no methods which are able to surpass this one.

Now, the [*Amitābha*] *Sutra* states that if one possesses but little goodness, one may fail to achieve that rebirth, whereas, if one has accumulated much merit, one may then succeed in arriving there. If one wishes to discuss "much merit," then there is no means for gaining it which can compare with upholding that [buddha's] name. If one wishes to speak of "goodness," then there is nothing which can compare with generating the vastly magnanimous resolve.

Thus it is that if one were to practice maintaining mindfulness of that ārya's name only for a brief period, that would be superior to cultivating the practice of giving for a full hundred years. If one were to generate the great resolve but one time, that would allow one to leap beyond the progress gained from passing through eons of prior cultivation.

Now as for mindfulness of the Buddha, its very root is the aspiration to become a buddha. Thus, if one fails to generate the great resolve, then, even though one might carry on the practice of mindfulness, how could one expect to succeed?

As for generating the resolve, its source lies with cultivating the practices. Were one to fail to achieve rebirth in the Pureland, then, although one might actually generate that resolve, still, it could be easy to retreat from it. Thus it is that, when one plants the seed of bodhi, one then tills [the mind ground] with the plow of mindfulness-of-the-Buddha. As a result, the fruit of the Path naturally develops and grows.

When one climbs aboard the ship of great vows, one then succeeds in entering the seas of the Pureland and then definitely gains rebirth in that region in the West. This is the ninth of the causal bases for generation of the bodhi resolve.

10. Causing Right Dharma to Endure for a Long Time

What is meant by "causing right Dharma to endure for a long time"? This refers to the fact that, from countless kalpas ago right on to

为我等故。修菩提道。难行
能行。难忍能忍。因圆果
满。遂致成佛。既成佛已。
化缘周讫。入于涅盘。正法
像法。皆已灭尽。仅存末
法。有教无人。邪正不分。
是非莫辨。竞争人我。尽逐
利名。举目滔滔。天下皆
是。不知佛是何人。法是何
义。僧是何名。衰残至此。
殆不忍言。每一思及。不觉
泪下。我为佛子。不能报
恩。内无益于己。外无益于
人。生无益于时。死无益于
后。天虽高不能覆我。地虽
厚不能载我。极重罪人。非
我而谁。由是痛不可忍。计
无所出。顿忘鄙陋。忽发大
心。虽不能挽回末运于此
时。决当图护持正法于来世

為我等故。修菩提道。難行
能行。難忍能忍。因圓果
滿。遂致成佛。既成佛已。
化緣周訖。入於涅槃。正法
像法。皆已滅盡。僅存末
法。有教無人。邪正不分。
是非莫辨。競爭人我。盡逐
利名。舉目滔滔。天下皆
是。不知佛是何人。法是何
義。僧是何名。衰殘至此。
殆不忍言。每一思及。不覺
淚下。我為佛子。不能報
恩。內無益於己。外無益於
人。生無益於時。死無益於
後。天雖高不能覆我。地雖
厚不能載我。極重罪人。非
我而誰。由是痛不可忍。計
無所出。頓忘鄙陋。忽發大
心。雖不能挽回末運於此
時。決當圖護持正法於來世

简体字   正體字

the present, our Bhagavān cultivated the bodhi path for our sakes. He was able to practice what is difficult to practice. He was able to endure what is difficult to endure. The cause became perfect and the fruit of it became full. Consequently, he arrived at the achievement of buddhahood. Having succeeded in achieving buddhahood and having then concluded his transforming those beings with whom he had affinities, he entered nirvāṇa.

Now, the Right Dharma Age and the Dharma Image Age have both entirely expired. There remains only the Dharma Ending Age wherein the Dharma continues to exist but there are no longer people [embodying realization of Dharma]. The deviant and the correct are no longer distinguished. Right and wrong are no longer discerned. Struggles proliferate between "them" and "us." People are entirely devoted to chasing after prosperity and fame. Wherever one looks, we are inundated with such people. The entire world has become this way.

People now do not even recognize who "the Buddha" is; they do not recognize what is meant by the word "Dharma" and they do not realize what is designated by the term "Sangha." Matters have now deteriorated to such a miserable state that one can barely bear to speak of this. Whenever one starts to reflect upon it, tears stream down spontaneously.

If, as a son of the Buddha, I am unable to repay such kindness—inwardly, there shall be no benefit for one's self and outwardly, there shall be no benefit for others. It shall then be the case that, while alive, one provides no benefit to anyone during this era and, after one's death, one affords no benefit to those who come along afterwards.

In such a case, though the heavens may extend high above, still, they remain unable to give me cover. Though the earth may be massive, it remains unable to support me. Then, if "a person possessed of the most extremely grave karmic crimes" does not apply to me, to whom could it even be applied at all?

On account of this, one feels unbearable pain and discerns that there would be no way to escape [from this indictment]. Suddenly, one forgets one's inferior qualities and then immediately generates the great resolve. Then, although one remains unable to turn back the Dharma-ending process dominating this era, one nonetheless remains determined that he will strive to guard and maintain right Dharma throughout one's future lifetimes.

是故偕诸善友。同到道场。
述为忏摩。建兹法会。发四
十八之大愿。愿愿度生。期
百千劫之深心。心心作佛。
从于今日。尽未来际。毕此
一形。誓归安养。既登九品
回入娑婆。俾得佛日重辉。
法门再阐。僧海澄清于此
界。人民被化于东方。劫运
为之更延。正法得以久住。
此则区区真实苦心。是为发
菩提心第十因缘也。如是十
缘备识。八法周知。则趣向
有门。开发有地。相与得此
人身。居于华夏。六根无
恙。四大轻安。具有信心。
幸无魔障。况今我等又得出
家。又受具戒。又遇道场。
又闻佛法。又瞻舍利。又修
忏法。

是故偕諸善友。同到道場。
述為懺摩。建茲法會。發四
十八之大願。願願度生。期
百千劫之深心。心心作佛。
從於今日。盡未來際。畢此
一形。誓歸安養。既登九品
回入娑婆。俾得佛日重輝。
法門再闡。僧海澄清於此
界。人民被化於東方。劫運
為之更延。正法得以久住。
此則區區真實苦心。是為發
菩提心第十因緣也。如是十
緣備識。八法周知。則趣向
有門。開發有地。相與得此
人身。居於華夏。六根無
恙。四大輕安。具有信心。
幸無魔障。況今我等又得出
家。又受具戒。又遇道場。
又聞佛法。又瞻舍利。又修
懺法。

简体字　　　正體字

Consequently, joined together with friends devoted to goodness, one arrives along with them at a *bodhimaṇḍala* (a temple or monastery) and arranges the convening of a *kṣama* assembly.[36] Having set up this Dharma assembly, one then makes the forty-eight great vows wherein each and every vow is devoted to bringing beings across to liberation. One sets forth the profound resolve which endures for a hundred thousand kalpas and which, in thought after thought, is devoted to becoming a buddha, making this vow effective, "from this very day onward to the very end of future time."

One vows that, when this physical body meets its end, one will return to [the land of] "peace and sustenance"[37] and, having ascended through the nine classes [of lotus abodes],[38] one shall return into this Sahā World[39] so that the sun of buddhahood will manifest its shining glory here yet again, so that gateways into Dharma will be expounded once more, so that this world's Sangha sea will be clarified, so that the populations of these eastern regions[40] will receive the transforming teachings, so that the era before the arrival of the inevitable will become extended by this, and so that right Dharma will thus be caused to endure for a long time.

This then is what I humbly set forth here in the way of genuinely-felt and patiently-enduring resolve. This is the tenth of the causal bases for generation of the bodhi resolve.

III. The Concluding Section

Thus it is that the ten conditions may be well recognized and the eight dharmas completely understood. Having accomplished this, one now possesses the gateways through which one can set forth and possesses the grounds upon which one may initiate generation [of the bodhi resolve].

Additionally, one has gotten this human body, dwells here in the domain of Chinese civilization [wherein the Dharma flourishes], possesses the six sense faculties free of any impairment, and enjoys [physical health supported by] the four great elements abiding in a state of light easefulness. One has equipped oneself with a faith-filled mind and has the great good fortune to be free of demon-inflicted obstacles.

This is all the more true for those of us who have also left behind the householder's life, have also gained the precepts of complete ordination, have also encountered a *bodhimaṇḍala*, have also heard the Buddha's Dharma explained, have also personally viewed the *śarīra*, have also cultivated the dharma of repentance, have also met

又值善友。又具胜缘。不于
今日发此大心。更待何日。
唯愿大众。愍我愚诚。怜我
苦志。同立此愿。同发是
心。未发者今发。已发者增
长。已增长者今令相续。勿
畏难而退怯。勿视易而轻
浮。勿欲速而不久长。勿懈
怠而无勇猛。勿委靡而不振
起。勿因循而更期待。勿因
愚钝而一向无心。勿以根浅
而自鄙无分。譬诸种树。种
久则根浅而日深。又如磨
刀。磨久则刀钝而成利。岂
可因浅勿种。任其自枯。因
钝弗磨。置之无用。又若以
修行为苦。则不知懈怠尤
苦。修行则勤劳暂时。安乐
永劫。懈怠则偷安一世。受
苦多生。况乎以净土为舟
航。则何愁退转。又

又值善友。又具勝緣。不於
今日發此大心。更待何日。
唯願大眾。愍我愚誠。憐我
苦志。同立此願。同發是
心。未發者今發。已發者增
長。已增長者今令相續。勿
畏難而退怯。勿視易而輕
浮。勿欲速而不久長。勿懈
怠而無勇猛。勿委靡而不振
起。勿因循而更期待。勿因
愚鈍而一向無心。勿以根淺
而自鄙無分。譬諸種樹。種
久則根淺而日深。又如磨
刀。磨久則刀鈍而成利。豈
可因淺勿種。任其自枯。因
鈍弗磨。置之無用。又若以
修行為苦。則不知懈怠尤
苦。修行則勤勞暫時。安樂
永劫。懈怠則偷安一世。受
苦多生。況乎以淨土為舟
航。則何愁退轉。又

简体字

正體字

up with the good [spiritual] friend, and have also become entirely equipped with the superior conditions for success. [Having now gained such a propitious circumstance], if one does not now on this very day proceed to generate this great resolve, then for which more suitable day [could one possibly] be waiting?

I only pray that the Great Assembly will take pity on this foolish display of sincerity, will feel sympathy for my deeply-felt resolve, will join together in setting forth these vows, and will unite in generating this [bodhi] resolve.

Those who have not generated it may now generate it. Those who have already generated it may now cause it to develop more fully. Those who have already caused it to develop more fully may now cause it to remain perpetually manifest.

Do not, fearing difficulty, shrink back in timidity. Do not, regarding this matter as easy, take it but lightly. Do not, seeking a swift conclusion, fail to make a long-enduring commitment. Do not, through indolence, remain bereft of heroic bravery. Do not, on account of being shiftless and spiritless, fail to incite yourself to bold action. Do not, drifting along in customary fashion, continue to put it off for another time. Do not, judging yourself to be foolish and dull-witted, continue depriving yourself of resolve. Do not, possessing only shallow roots [of goodness], judge yourself to be an inferior person with no share in this.

This endeavor is analogous to the planting of a tree. Once planted, those roots, once shallow, grow deeper each day. This is also analogous to the sharpening of a knife. When one has honed it for a while, that knife, once dull, becomes sharp.

How could one, on account of shallow [roots], fail to plant [the tree], thus allowing it to dry up [and die]? How could one, on account of the [knife's] dullness, just set it aside and stop using it?

Additionally, if one regards cultivation to be a form of suffering, then one fails to realize that indolence entails even *more* suffering. In the case of cultivation, one need only be temporarily devoted to diligent effort. Afterwards, one enjoys peace and bliss for an eternity of kalpas. In the case of indolence, one may steal a single lifetime of peacefulness, but then be bound to undergo many lifetimes in suffering.

How much the more so is this the case when one employs the Pureland as a ship [to one's destination]. What worries could there be that one might retreat from [one's quest]? Additionally, once

得无生为忍力。则何虑艰
难。当知地狱罪人。尚发菩
提于往劫。岂可人伦佛子。
不立大愿于今生。无始昏
迷。往者既不可谏。而今觉
悟。将来犹尚可追。然迷而
未悟。固可哀怜。苟知而不
行。尤为痛惜。若惧地狱之
苦。则精进自生。若念无常
之速。则懈怠不起。又须以
佛法为鞭策。善友为提携。
造次弗离。终身依赖。则无
退失之虞矣。勿言一念轻
微。勿谓虚愿无益。心真则
事实。愿广则行深。虚空非
大。心王为大。金刚非坚。
愿力最坚。大众诚能不弃我
语。则菩提眷属。从而联
姻。莲社宗盟。自今缔好。
所愿同生净土。同见弥陀。
同化众生。同成正觉。

得無生為忍力。則何慮艱
難。當知地獄罪人。尚發菩
提於往劫。豈可人倫佛子。
不立大願於今生。無始昏
迷。往者既不可諫。而今覺
悟。將來猶尚可追。然迷而
未悟。固可哀憐。苟知而不
行。尤為痛惜。若懼地獄之
苦。則精進自生。若念無常
之速。則懈怠不起。又須以
佛法為鞭策。善友為提攜。
造次弗離。終身依賴。則無
退失之虞矣。勿言一念輕
微。勿謂虛願無益。心真則
事實。願廣則行深。虛空非
大。心王為大。金剛非堅。
願力最堅。大眾誠能不棄我
語。則菩提眷屬。從而聯
姻。蓮社宗盟。自今締好。
所願同生淨土。同見彌陀。
同化眾生。同成正覺。

简体字   正體字

one gains realization of the unproduced [dharmas patience] as the source of one's power of endurance, what concerns could remain about any difficulties?

One should realize that even those karmic transgressors in the hells generated the bodhi resolve at some point in kalpas past. How then could a son of the Buddha sharing in the social order of humans somehow fail to make the great vows in this present life?

All across the course of beginningless time we have been immersed in confusion. Although one cannot plead [for changes] regarding one's past, nonetheless, were one to awaken now, one might still hope to change the course of the future. As for those who abide in confusion and have not yet awakened, one certainly finds them pitiable. However, it is only in a case where someone comprehends [the situation] but still fails to act that one is moved to feel especially deep regret.

Were one to feel terror over the sufferings of the hells, vigorous effort would naturally arise. Were one to become mindful of the swiftness of the effects of impermanence, indolence would not manifest. Additionally, it is essential to employ the Buddha's Dharma as one might use an instigating whip and to avail oneself of the good [spiritual] friend as a source of assistance. If one were to refrain from carelessly separating from them, but rather continued such reliance for one's entire life, then there would be no danger of retreating and losing one's way.

Do not claim that a single thought is insignificant. Do not hold the opinion that "empty vows" are devoid of any benefit. If one's mind abides in truth, then one's endeavors will be genuine. If one's vows are vast in their scope, then one's practice will be profound. It is not the case that empty space qualifies as great. Rather it is the mind king which qualifies as great. It is not the case that *vajra*[41] really qualifies as durable. Rather it is the power of vows which is most durable.

If the Great Assembly is truly able to refrain from casting aside my pronouncements, then, based on this, a congregation destined towards bodhi may join together. Thus the alliance of a lotus society may be formally initiated from this very time.

As for what we have vowed to achieve, it is for all of us together to gain rebirth in the Pureland, for all of us together to see Amitābha Buddha, for all of us together to engage in the teaching of beings, and for all of us together to perfect the right enlightenment.

则安知未来三十二相。百福庄岩。不从今日发心立愿而始也。愿与大众共勉之。幸甚幸甚。	則安知未來三十二相。百福莊巖。不從今日發心立願而始也。願與大眾共勉之。幸甚幸甚。
简体字	正體字

This being the case, how can one know that our future attainment of the thirty-two marks with their hundred-fold adornment of merit is not a result inaugurated on this very day by this generating of the [bodhi] resolve and by this declaration of vows?

I wish now to offer encouragement to everyone in the Great Assembly. This is so extremely fortunate—so extremely fortunate!

Part Two Endnotes

1. "Great Assembly" is a standard designation referring to the monks, nuns, laymen, and laywomen comprising any given Buddhist congregation.

2. Since "bodhi" means "enlightenment," "bodhi resolve" (Sanskrit: *bodhicitta*) means "the mind determined to gain enlightenment." This refers to the formal commitment to the firm resolution that one will strive ceaselessly to gain the utmost, right, and perfect enlightenment of a buddha, doing so for the sake of liberating all beings from the sufferings of cyclic existence.

3. This quotation is found both in the 60-fascicle translation of Buddhabhadra (T9.278.663a) and the 80-fascicle translation of Śikṣānanda (T10.279.307c) as part of the "Transcending the World" Chapter (*Li shijian pin*: 離世間品). The context is as the first member of a list of ten types of demonic karmic activity following upon a list of ten literal and figurative "demons." It stands right before a list of ten means for abandoning demonic karma.

4. "Tathāgata" is an alternate honorific designation for a buddha translated into Chinese as "Thus Come One" (如來). In a list of ten alternate designations of a buddha, "Tathāgata" is the first.

5. "Bodhisattva" means "enlightenment being." It specifically refers to someone who has vowed to become a fully-enlightened buddha by completing the Bodhisattva Path to that goal. The fundamental "bodhisattva vow" is what is commonly termed "generation of the bodhi resolve (*bodhicitta*)."

6. "Cyclic birth-and-death" is the condition to which all beings are subject. This refers to the process of ceaseless rebirth throughout the "six destinies" of the gods, demi-gods, humans, animals, hungry ghosts, and hells. It is a process ruled by cause-and-effect as mediated by the quality of our karmic actions of body, mouth, and mind. The Buddha identified this process as inextricably bound up with inevitable sufferings which may only be transcended through enlightenment.

7. In Buddhism, a "stupa" is a typically multi-storied memorial to a holy being or sacred site.

8. "*Śarīra*" are the often jewel-like "relics" which remain in the ashes resulting from the cremation of particularly holy beings. The author refers here to the relics of the Buddha himself, some of which were present right there in Hangzhou during his own lifetime.

9. This is a classical filial-piety literature idiom referring to maternal sacrifices in attending to infants.

10. "Śramaṇa" is one of the designations commonly used for fully-

ordained Buddhist monks.

11. This is a euphemistic way of saying, "no different from animals."

12. This refers to the bhikshu's outer robe, the mark of the higher ordination conferred by the Buddha's celibate monastic orders.

13. "Lesser sorts of fruits of the Path" is a reference to the option to seek the individual-enlightenment goal of arhatship instead of the universal-enlightenment option of the bodhisattva's path to complete buddhahood.

14. This is a classical idiom referring to residences of the very poor.

15. "The two adornments" of merit and wisdom refers to the two fundamental requirements for the achievement of buddhahood.

16. *Dāna*, the first of the six perfections, is the Buddhist Sanskrit term for "giving." In practice, it refers specifically to offerings made to fully-ordained members of the Buddha's monastic community (the Sangha). It is a fundamental teaching of Buddhism that such giving is generative of karmic "merit" for the benefactors. Such merit is the resource from which greater happiness and better fortune may be expected to arise in the future, this as a direct consequence of the karmic "goodness" of the action performed. The amount of merit generated bears a direct relationship to the karmic purity and path-refinement of the recipients of such giving.

17. This "coming back together" and this "coming to life again" are but means to make hell-sufferer available again for continued infliction of retributive torture.

18. In Buddhism, "Yama" is the king of the dead who, upon one's death, reviews one's karmic record and, based on the quality of one's earthly deeds, directs one to the appropriate reward or retribution. One may think of King Yama as a sort of metaphoric and anthropomorphic stand-in for the law of karma.

19. In his commentary on this work (勸發菩提心文講義), the immensely learned and eloquent Dharma Master Yuanying (圓瑛大師: 1878–1953) explained that this refers to an actual case involving a rural family which raised donkeys in Jingeng County (金耕縣), close to Nanjing. (I paraphrase Master Yuanying's explanation below.)

    The mother had died when the son was only three years old, had a history of no particularly good karma, and happened on that account to fall into the realm of animals where she was reborn as a donkey in her very own former household (this most likely to repay some of her own former exploitation of donkey labor). By the time the story is told, her tenure as a donkey had already extended to sixteen years.

    The donkey happened to be returning one day, bearing a load of grain, but now being old for a donkey, was moving very slowly, much to the irritation of the young man who had been her son. He then became so angry that he whipped her till she bled, whereupon the donkey turned back its head towards him and cried out in pain. It is because the son had no idea that the donkey had been his mother, that the text states: "Who could know, 'This is the anguish of my own mother'?"

That very night, the spirit of the donkey came to the son in a vivid dream, reporting, "I'm your former mother who, on account of having formerly taken four taels of silver from your father, took rebirth as a donkey to repay the debt. Now, however, that karmic "debt" has been entirely repaid, so you should no longer cause me pain with that whip." The son awoke in a fright and, being fearful of ever exploiting the donkey again, raised it as one would a pet.

20. In the same commentary, Master Yuanying explains this reference to the pain of the pig as one which involved a pig-butchering family in Huangyen County (黃岩縣) Zhejiang Province. When on the verge of butchering a very large pig, it came in a dream to the pig-owner's previous-life son, revealing its former identity as his father. Again, the son immediately desisted from carrying through with the slaughter and instead raised the animal as a pet.

21. King Wen of the Zhou Dynasty was reputed to be a great sage. Tradition has it that a great sage would be able to recognize if he was being served the flesh of his own son. Thus it was that King Wen was tricked into eating the flesh of one of his hundred sons to test whether this was true.

22. Literally "flesh and bones."

23. "Ten months" is based on referencing the lunar calendar as the operative standard.

24. A "chiliocosm" is a vast world system, only one of the countless number of inhabited world systems populating Buddhist cosmology.

25. "The three wretched destinies" is a reference to the realms of the hungry ghosts, the animals, and the hells.

26. This is an alternate honorific designation for a buddha which Chinese translators render as "World Honored One." In a list of ten alternate designations of a buddha, "Bhagavān" is number ten.

27. A *duṣkṛta* precept is one of the most minor of the rules and regulations required of a fully-ordained monk or nun.

28. *Niraya* is an alternate designation for the hells.

29. Master Yuanying notes in his commentary that this equals nine million years in the realm of humans.

30. *Śīla*, the second of the six perfections, is the Buddhist Sanskrit designation for moral virtue in general and the various codes of moral

virtue in particular.

31. An *upāsaka* is a Buddhist layman, specifically one who has, at mini-mum, formally taken the Three Refuges (in the Buddha, in the Dharma, and in the āryā [enlightened] Sangha). The five precepts (the minimal moral standards for insuring at least a human rebirth) proscribe kill-ing, stealing, sexual misconduct, lying, and intoxicants.

32. A *śrāmaṇera* is a novice monk.

33. A "bhikshu" (Sanskrit: *bhikṣu*) is a fully-ordained Buddhist monk. As decreed by Shākyamuni Buddha himself, only fully-ordained celi-bates upholding a moral code of approximately 250 regulations laid down by the Buddha himself are to be regarded as genuine Buddhist clergy.

34. The "Pureland" refers to the buddhaland of Amitābha Buddha in which, through making vows to do so, one may gain rebirth. Due to the absence of obstructive obstacles and negative conditions so typi-cal of this Sahā world, Amitābha's buddhaland is widely recognized in Mahāyāna Buddhism to be a much easier place to achieve dramatic advancement in the career of a bodhisattva.

 Two doctrinal concepts may help the uninitiated reconcile this seemingly "celestial" destination with the rest of Buddhist doctrine: First, the essence of the Pureland is the pure mind which, even there, must be developed through individually-cultivated effort. Second, achievement of rebirth in the Pureland does not relieve the aspirant to buddhahood of the need to return in due course to the work of liberating other beings from karma-bound suffering associated with cyclic births and deaths in the six rebirth destinies.

35. In Buddhism, the Sanskrit word *ārya* refers to those who have suc-ceeded in reaching what is termed "the path of seeing." This involves, among other things, gaining a direct perception of the reality of the mind and the world as it really is when stripped of our delusion-bound obscurations and imputations. This is referred to in some tra-ditions as "seeing emptiness directly." ("Emptiness" is a shorthand designation for the "absence of inherent existence" in any and all phe-nomena.)

36. A *kṣama* assembly is a Dharma meeting wherein one asks forgiveness of transgressions. See *Foguang Dictionary*: p. 6774.

37. In the Sino-Buddhist tradition, "[The land of] peace and sustenance" is an alternate designation for the Pureland of Amitābha Buddha. Hirakawa's *Buddhist Chinese-Sanskrit Dictionary* corroborates (p. 375a) that 安養 was indeed one of the various Sino-Buddhist approaches for rendering the *sukha* (English: "blissful") of Sukhāvatī.

38. The nine classes of lotus abodes correspond to varying levels of

residence in the Pureland of Amitābha which correlate with one's level of accomplishment in the cultivation of the Buddhist Path.

39. "Sahā World" is a designation for the world with which we are all familiar, the world ruled by the afflictions of attachment, aversion, and delusion and which is characterized by a ceaseless transit up and down through the six destinies of rebirth, sometimes enjoying a blissful (but temporary) celestial existence, sometimes grinding along in the realm of human rebirth, and sometimes stopping in for awesomely-long periods of time to deal with heavy karmic debts in the purgatorial realms of hell. The Sahā world is defined in the Sino-Buddhist tradition as the world which is "difficult to bear."

40. "Eastern regions" are here termed "eastern" not in contrast to London, Paris, or New York, but rather to Amitābha's land of ultimate bliss, conventionally designated as being off in a westerly direction.

41. *Vājra*, often conventionally translated as "diamond" or "adamantine," is reputed to be the most ultimately solid and durable of substances.

Part Three:

EXHORTATION
to
RESOLVE ON BUDDHAHOOD

By the Tang Dynasty Literatus & Prime Minister Peixiu
(797–870 CE)

Preface by Huayan & Dhyāna Patriarch Śramaṇa Guifeng Zongmi
(780–840 CE)

Part Three Contents

Peixiu's Exhortation to Resolve on Buddhahood

CBETA V1.8
No. 1010
X58.1010.485c03–489b06

劝发菩提心文序。

终南山艸堂寺圭峰沙门宗密撰。

发菩提心者。崇德广业虚心外身圆觉之谓也。自非达恢廓之道。禀仁恕之性。怀远大之志者。其谁能发斯意焉。岂其如来灭后。后五百岁佛法衰。末世人少信。时有儒门上士河东裴公而当此仁。吾与裴公交佛道久已。知其入佛门到佛境及览劝发菩提心文。知其为佛使行佛事。吾为佛子宁不感之而踊跃乎。凡归佛者可宝之为龟镜。然佛门难入。失在偏邪。佛境难到。失在怠速。心外求法或身中计我邪也。唯尚理性或但宗因缘。偏也。持解迷行或沈空住寂。怠也。

简体字

CBETA V1.8
No. 1010
X58.1010.485c03–489b06

勸發菩提心文序。

終南山艸堂寺圭峰沙門宗密撰。

發菩提心者。崇德廣業虛心外身圓覺之謂也。自非達恢廓之道。稟仁恕之性。懷遠大之志者。其誰能發斯意焉。豈其如來滅後。後五百歲佛法衰。末世人少信。時有儒門上士河東裴公而當此仁。吾與裴公交佛道久已。知其入佛門到佛境及覽勸發菩提心文。知其為佛使行佛事。吾為佛子寧不感之而踊躍乎。凡歸佛者可寶之為龜鏡。然佛門難入。失在偏邪。佛境難到。失在怠速。心外求法或身中計我邪也。唯尚理性或但宗因緣。偏也。持解迷行或沈空住寂。怠也。

正體字

Dhyāna Master Zongmi's Original Preface

By Śramaṇa Guifeng Zongmi of Zhongnan Mountain's Caotang Monastery

As for generating the bodhi resolve, it is a matter of towering virtue, vastness of karmic deeds, bringing emptiness to one's mind, and treating one's body as merely external. This is as stated in the *Perfect Enlightenment Sutra*. If one has not penetrated through to the path of magnanimity and expansiveness, been endowed with a nature inclined towards humanity and empathy, and also equipped oneself with a far-reaching and grand resoluteness, who would be able to generate this resolve?

Could it be that, in the final five hundred years after the Tathāgata's cessation, when the Buddha Dharma has deteriorated to its endpoint and only a few men of the world maintain faith in it, there now appears this superior Confucian eminence, the noble Pei from east of the River, who has taken on this sort of humanity?

For a long time now, I have been linked up with the noble Pei on the Buddhist path. I had become aware that he had entered the Buddha's gateway and arrived at the mind state of the Buddha. When I came to the point of examining his "Exhortation to Resolve on Buddhahood," I realized right then that he is an emissary of the Buddha engaged in carrying on the Buddha's work. How could I, as a son of the Buddha, not be overcome with gratitude and leap up in delight?

Whosoever has taken the Refuges with the Buddha may treasure it as [an exemplary standard] comparable to the turtle-[shell oracle or reflecting] mirror.[1] Now, the gateway of the Buddha is difficult to enter into. One may miss it either through one-sided biases or through straying into deviation. The Buddha's state of mind is difficult to reach. One may miss it through being inclined towards either indolence or haste.

If one seeks for the Dharma outside of the mind or if one reckons the existence of a self within this body, then these are instances of deviation. If one is solely oriented towards the noumenal nature or if one only venerates causes and conditions as one's lineage bases, then these are instances of bias.

If one holds to an [intellectual] understanding while remaining deluded about the practice or, alternately, if one becomes submerged in emptiness and abides in stillness, these are instances of indolence.

简体字	正體字
劳形苦神而克期待证。速也。今裴公所得所行所演所劝。佥异于是。所谓洞了自心。德等于佛。非心外求也。洞了形识。空如幻化。非自计我。真如本觉。是其所宗。非但缘也。四谛六度。是其所弘。非唯性也。礼供赞念。率身励人。非速行也。福智悲愿。孜孜是务。非沈住也。气和神适。乘缘应事。非劳苦也。以时消息。为而不待。非求证也。如是备众德。离诸病。非入佛门到佛境何耶。吾久同其愿又览其文咏歌。不足故辄为序。今而后有欲入佛门造佛境者。宜信受奉行。	勞形苦神而剋期待證。速也。今裴公所得所行所演所勸。僉異於是。所謂洞了自心。德等於佛。非心外求也。洞了形識。空如幻化。非自計我。真如本覺。是其所宗。非但緣也。四諦六度。是其所弘。非唯性也。禮供讚念。率身勵人。非速行也。福智悲願。孜孜是務。非沈住也。氣和神適。乘緣應事。非勞苦也。以時消息。為而不待。非求證也。如是備眾德。離諸病。非入佛門到佛境何耶。吾久同其願又覽其文詠歌。不足故輒為序。今而後有欲入佛門造佛境者。宜信受奉行。

If one exhausts the physical body or subjects the spirit to bitter suffering, and by doing so, one seeks to set an appointed time for the arrival of realizations, these are instances of hastiness.

Now, that which the noble Pei has realized, that which he practices, that which he proclaims, and that which he encourages are of an entirely different order from such issues.

As for what is termed "utterly comprehending one's own mind and achieving meritorious qualities the equal of the Buddha," these are not instances of seeking outside of one's own mind. When one penetrates through to utter comprehension that physical forms and consciousness are empty and like an illusory conjuration, this is not an instance of reckoning the existence of a self.

True suchness and original enlightenment constitute that which he reveres as lineage bases. This is not an instance of solely[2] looking to conditions. The four truths and the six perfections are what he promotes. This is not a case of focusing on "nature" alone.

Engaging in expressions of reverence, making offerings, singing praises, reciting [scripture], and leading through personal example while exhorting others—these are not instances of haste-based practice. Diligently taking on as a matter of duty these matters of merit, wisdom, compassion, and vows—this is not an instance of being submerged [in emptiness] or abiding [in stillness].

Maintaining harmony of one's energies and adaptability of one's spirit while according with conditions in responding to situations—this is not a case of exhausting [the physical body] or [subjecting the spirit to] bitter suffering. Allowing oneself to rest when the time is right while engaging in the practice without waiting [expectantly]—this is not an instance of seeking after realizations.

To perfect the manifold meritorious qualities in this fashion while abandoning all faults—if this is not a case of entering the gateway of the Buddha and arriving in the realm of the Buddha, what is it?

I have for a long time now already resolved on the very same vows as he has. Moreover, having perused his essay, I find that "chanting and singing are insufficient to express one's feelings about it."[3] It is for this reason that, at my own behest, I produced a preface for it. Now and in the future, where there are those who wish to enter the gateway of the Buddha and create for themselves the realm of a buddha, it is only appropriate that they faithfully accept this work and uphold its tenets in their practice.

普劝僧俗发菩提心文。

唐相国裴休述。

普告大众。若僧若俗。有能同发阿耨多罗三藐三菩提心者。我愿生生常为道俗。同宗同趣。同愿同求。同运大悲。同修大智。递相辅助。直至菩提。普告大众。若僧若俗。有能同发阿耨多罗三藐三菩提心者。我愿生生常同净业。各领眷属。分化众生。龙华会中。同受佛记。广修大愿。直至菩提。

初明菩提名义。

阿耨多罗三藐三菩提者。此云无上正遍知觉。

（无上者。究竟也。正者。如理知遍者。无量智正觉知真俗智。）

是诸佛所证最上妙道。是众生所迷根本妙源。既慕如来永离诸苦。自悲己身久失大利。慨然奋发将求佛身。即是初发阿耨多罗三藐三菩提心也。

简体字

普勸僧俗發菩提心文。

唐相國裴休述。

普告大眾。若僧若俗。有能同發阿耨多羅三藐三菩提心者。我願生生常為道俗。同宗同趣。同願同求。同運大悲。同修大智。遞相輔助。直至菩提。普告大眾。若僧若俗。有能同發阿耨多羅三藐三菩提心者。我願生生常同淨業。各領眷屬。分化眾生。龍華會中。同受佛記。廣修大願。直至菩提。

初明菩提名義。

阿耨多羅三藐三菩提者。此云無上正遍知覺。

（無上者。究竟也。正者。如理知遍者。無量智正覺知真俗智。）

是諸佛所證最上妙道。是眾生所迷根本妙源。既慕如來永離諸苦。自悲己身久失大利。慨然奮發將求佛身。即是初發阿耨多羅三藐三菩提心也。

正體字

An Exhortation for All Sangha and Laity
To Resolve on Buddhahood

By the Tang Dynasty Prime Minister Peixiu

Let it be known throughout the Great Community[4] that, whether Sangha or laity, where there are those who are able to unite in generating the resolve to realize *anuttarasamyaksaṃbodhi*, I vow that, in life-after-life, for the sake of both Sangha and laity, I shall always join in the same lineage,[5] in the same pathway,[6] in the same vows, in the same aspirations, in the same implementation of the great compassion, and in the same cultivation of the great wisdom as we mutually assist each other in progressing directly on through to realization of bodhi.

Let it be known throughout the Great Community that, whether Sangha or laity, where there are those who are able to unite in generating the resolve to realize *anuttarasamyaksaṃbodhi*, I vow that, in life-after-life, I will always join with them in performing the same pure karmic works as we each lead forth followers and each separately engage in the transformative teaching of beings. We shall join together again in the Dragon Flower Assembly[7] to receive predictions of buddhahood and then shall continue on to extensively cultivate great vows, doing so directly on through to the realization of bodhi.

Explanation of the Term "Bodhi"

As for [the term] *anuttarasamyaksaṃbodhi*, this means "the unsurpassed, right, and universal enlightenment."

> **Interlinear note:** "Unsurpassed" means "ultimate." "Right" means "knowing that accords with the noumenal."[8] "Universal" refers to "immeasurable wisdom." "Right enlightenment" refers to "wisdom which knows [both] the genuine and the conventional [truths]."

It is the most supreme and marvelous path realized by all buddhas and it is the original marvelous source about which beings are deluded. Having admired the Tathāgata's eternal separation from all suffering and having been saddened by having long lost the great benefit oneself, one earnestly resolves with abundant spirit that one will strive to gain the body of a buddha. It is this which constitutes the initial generation of the resolve to realize *anuttarasamyaksaṃbodhi*.

次明菩提心体。

既发菩提大心。须识菩提心体。夫菩提心体不从真心发。无由得至菩提。故须拣择分明。方是正因法行。且大众从无始来常认为我身者是地水火风从合之身。旋聚旋散。属无常法。非我身也。大众从无始来常认为我心者是缘虑容尘虚妄之心。乍起乍灭。属无常法。非我心也。我有真身圆满空寂者是。我有真心广大灵知者是也。

（圆满者。法身无量功德本自具足也。空寂者。法身离诸色相永无动摇也。广大者。真心体兼法界包含虚空也。灵知者。了了分明鉴照清彻也。）

空寂灵智。神用自在。性含万德。体绝百非。如净月轮圆满无缺。惑云所覆不自

次明菩提心體。

既發菩提大心。須識菩提心體。夫菩提心體不從真心發。無由得至菩提。故須揀擇分明。方是正因法行。且大眾從無始來常認為我身者是地水火風從合之身。旋聚旋散。屬無常法。非我身也。大眾從無始來常認為我心者是緣慮容塵虛妄之心。乍起乍滅。屬無常法。非我心也。我有真身圓滿空寂者是。我有真心廣大靈知者是也。

（圓滿者。法身無量功德本自具足也。空寂者。法身離諸色相永無動搖也。廣大者。真心體兼法界包含虛空也。靈知者。了了分明鑒照清徹也。）

空寂靈智。神用自在。性含萬德。體絕百非。如淨月輪圓滿無缺。惑雲所覆不自

简体字   正體字

Explanation of the Essence of the Bodhi Mind

Having generated the great mind to realize bodhi, it is necessary to recognize what constitutes the essence of the bodhi mind. Now, as for the substance of the bodhi mind, if one fails to generate it from one's true mind, there is no source through which one might succeed in reaching bodhi. On account of this, it is essential that one differentiate clearly [what it is]. Only then does this result in Dharma practice which corresponds to correct causality.

Moreover, as for that which those in the Great Community have throughout beginningless time always recognized as "my body," it is a body consisting in an artificial conjunction of the earth, water, fire, and air elements. It comes together quickly but then soon disperses. It belongs to the sphere of impermanent dharmas. It does not qualify as "my" body.

As for that which those in the Great Community have recognized as "my mind," it is but an empty and false mind which is concerned with thinking about sense-object phenomena.[8] It suddenly arises and then swiftly disappears. It belongs to the sphere of impermanent dharmas. It does not qualify as "my" mind.

That genuine body which we possess is the one which is perfect and complete, empty and quiescent. That genuine mind which we possess is the one which is vast in its magnitude and replete with spiritually intelligent awareness.

> **Interlinear note:** As for "perfect and complete," the Dharma body is fundamentally inherently replete with an incalculable number of meritorious qualities. As for "empty and quiescent," the Dharma body transcends all forms or characteristics and is eternally free of any movement or shaking.
>
> As for "vast in its magnitude," the substance of the true mind coincides in its expansiveness with the Dharma realm (*dharma-dhātu*). It envelopes and contains [even] empty space.
>
> As for "spiritually intelligent awareness," this refers to an utterly sharp and focused investigative illumination which is both clear and penetrating.

This empty and quiescent spiritually intelligent awareness[9] is sovereignly independent in its spiritual functions. In its very nature it encompasses the myriad meritorious qualities. In its very essence, it cuts off the hundred sorts of fallacies.[10] It is comparable to that pure disk of the moon which, round and full, is free of any defects. It becomes so obscured by the clouds of delusion that one fails to

简体字	正體字
觉知。妄惑既除。真心本净也。十方诸佛一切众生与我此心三无差别。此即菩提心体也。舍此不认。而认自身妄念。随死随生。与禽畜杂类比肩受苦。为丈夫者岂不羞哉。既发无上道心。当行大丈夫事。起三心立五誓。修一切助菩提法。以诸佛为师。以菩萨为侣。以六道众生为眷属。以生死烦恼为园林。誓尽未来济拔度脱。是则名为发阿耨多罗三藐三菩提心也。 次明三心。 一者大悲心。既悟自心。本无生灭。遂悲六道。枉受沈沦。己虽未证菩提。且愿众生解脱。 （即经云菩提心己。虽未度。愿度未度。老子云。圣人后其身身先。儒家云。仁者博施济众。先人后己三教皆同）。 于是广发同体大悲。尽未来行四摄法。摄彼众生。皆令	覺知。妄惑既除。真心本淨也。十方諸佛一切眾生與我此心三無差別。此即菩提心體也。捨此不認。而認自身妄念。隨死隨生。與禽畜雜類比肩受苦。為丈夫者豈不羞哉。既發無上道心。當行大丈夫事。起三心立五誓。修一切助菩提法。以諸佛為師。以菩薩為侶。以六道眾生為眷屬。以生死煩惱為園林。誓盡未來濟拔度脫。是則名為發阿耨多羅三藐三菩提心也。 次明三心。 一者大悲心。既悟自心。本無生滅。遂悲六道。枉受沈淪。己雖未證菩提。且願眾生解脫。 （即經云菩提心己。雖未度。願度未度。老子云。聖人後其身身先。儒家云。仁者博施濟眾。先人後己三教皆同）。 於是廣發同體大悲。盡未來行四攝法。攝彼眾生。皆令

be aware of it. Once one's error-freighted delusions have been banished, the true mind manifests its original purity.

The Buddhas of the ten directions, all beings, and this mind of mine—"in these three, there are no distinctions."[11] It is this which is identical with the essence of the bodhi mind. One forsakes this and, failing to recognize it, one instead recognizes [only] one's own false thoughts. Consequently one engages in a continual process of dying and being reborn again and thus endures suffering shoulder-to-shoulder with the various species of birds and beasts. How could it be that one who is truly a man would not feel shamed by this?

Having generated the mind resolved on the unsurpassed Path, one should take up the actions of a great man, bring forth the three types of mind, establish the five vows, cultivate all of the bodhi-assisting dharmas, take the Buddhas as one's gurus, take the Bodhisattvas as one's companions, take the beings in the six destinies as one's followers, take cyclic birth-and-death and afflictions as garden and grove, and vow that, to the very end of future time, one will carry on with rescuing, extricating, and liberating. It is this then which qualifies as generating the mind resolved on realization of *anuttarasamyaksaṃbodhi*.

Explanation of the Three Types of Mind

First, the greatly compassionate mind. Having awakened to the fact that one's own mind is originally free of production and destruction, one consequently feels compassion for those in the six destinies who have wrongly sunken away in them. Although one has not yet realized bodhi oneself,[12] still, one wishes that beings might be liberated.

> **Interlinear note:** In the scriptures, it is said, "The bodhi mind is such that, although one has not gained liberation oneself, one nonetheless wishes to liberate those who have not yet gained liberation."[13] The *Laozi* states, "The sage places his own person last and thus his own person becomes foremost."[14] The Confucian tradition states, "One who is endowed with humanity gives liberally to all, rescues the multitudes, places others first, and places himself last." The three teaching traditions are all the same in this respect.

In this [adoption of the compassionate mind], one generates with vast scope the "identical-substance" great compassion. Then, even to the exhaustion of future time, one implements the four means of attraction[15] to draw in those beings and cause them all to take

归真。同成佛道。此即大悲心也。二者大智心。既兴大智。誓度群品。品类既多。根器不同。即须广事诸佛。广学妙法。一一证入。转化众生。此即大智心也。三者大愿心。既欲广度众生。遂兴广大悲智。然心惟本净。久翳尘劳。习性难顿。销除法器。须资磨宝。自虑轮迴诸趣。不遇佛法胜缘。故发大愿。备修万行。行愿相资。犹如车翼。运行不退。直至菩提。此即大愿心也。

（华严经云。菩提心灯以大悲为油。大愿为炷。大智为光。）

然三心之中。大愿为主。常持悲智。以度群生。故初发心必先起愿。

歸真。同成佛道。此即大悲心也。二者大智心。既興大智。誓度群品。品類既多。根器不同。即須廣事諸佛。廣學妙法。一一證入。轉化眾生。此即大智心也。三者大願心。既欲廣度眾生。遂興廣大悲智。然心惟本淨。久翳塵勞。習性難頓。銷除法器。須資磨寶。自慮輪迴諸趣。不遇佛法勝緣。故發大願。備修萬行。行願相資。猶如車翼。運行不退。直至菩提。此即大願心也。

（華嚴經云。菩提心燈以大悲為油。大願為炷。大智為光。）

然三心之中。大願為主。常持悲智。以度群生。故初發心必先起願。

简体字　　　正體字

refuge in what is true, so that they all alike perfect the path to bud-dhahood. This is precisely what is intended by the mind of great compassion.

Second, the mind of great wisdom. Having let the great compassion flourish,[16] one vows to liberate the many categories of beings. Because the many categories of beings are so numerous, the respective faculties and potentials by which they might become "vessels" [for the retention of Dharma] are not all the same. Thus it becomes essential to undertake extensive service to the Buddhas and to undertake extensive study of the sublime Dharma. One then gains realization and entry into each and every one [of those dharmas] and subsequently turns back again to engage in transforming [the minds of] beings. This is precisely what is intended by the mind of great wisdom.

Third, the mind established in great vows. Since one aspires to engage in liberating beings on a vast scale, one consequently lets expansively great compassion and wisdom flourish. However, even though the mind is fundamentally pure, it has nonetheless long been obscured by one's toiling on amid the "dusts" of the sense objects. One's habitual propensities, by their very nature, are difficult to suddenly melt away. A vessel [for the retention] of Dharma is such that one must refine it through polishing and tempering.[17] One contemplates the prospect of coursing along in the destinies of cyclic existence while not encountering the superior conditions of the Buddha's Dharma. Consequently he generates great vows while also setting about comprehensively perfecting the cultivation of the myriad practices.[18] The practices and the vows mutually aid each other in just the same way as do [the two wheels of] a chariot or [the two] wings [of a bird]. Thus it is that one progresses along, does not retreat, and proceeds directly on through to the realization of bodhi. This is precisely what is intended by the mind established in great vows.

> **Interlinear note:** The *Floral Adornment Sutra* states: The lamp of the bodhi mind takes the great compassion as its oil, takes great vows as its wick,[19] and takes great wisdom as its illumination.

Now, among these three types of mind, it is the one committed to great vows which is primary. This is because it constantly supports the compassion and wisdom through which one liberates the many beings. Therefore, along with the initial generation of the [bodhi] resolve, one must necessarily first bring forth vows.

华严行愿经云。若人临命终时。最后刹那。一切诸根悉皆散坏。一切亲属悉皆舍离。一切威势悉皆退失。一切财宝无复相随。唯此愿王不相舍离。常为引导。直至菩提。是故汝等闻此愿王。莫生疑念。

（华严最后普贤所说。定非虚妄。依此修行）。

次明五誓。

一者众生无边誓愿度。二者福智无边誓愿集。三者佛法无边誓愿学。四者如来无边誓愿事。五者无上正觉誓愿成。持此五誓。念念运心。无有间断。是为具菩提大心。是为持菩提心戒。三心五誓重叠相资。佛佛道同不过于此。即是具足发阿耨多罗三藐三菩提心也。

次劝常持菩提心。

普告大众。若僧若俗。既已发菩提大心。修菩萨妙道。至诚普启诸佛。一心普摄众生。

华严行愿经云。若人临命终时。最後刹那。一切诸根悉皆散壞。一切親屬悉皆捨離。一切威势悉皆退失。一切财寶無復相随。唯此願王不相捨離。常為引導。直至菩提。是故汝等聞此願王。莫生疑念。

（華嚴最後普賢所說。定非虛妄。依此修行）。

次明五誓。

一者眾生無邊誓願度。二者福智無邊誓願集。三者佛法無邊誓願學。四者如來無邊誓願事。五者無上正覺誓願成。持此五誓。念念運心。無有間斷。是為具菩提大心。是為持菩提心戒。三心五誓重疊相資。佛佛道同不過於此。即是具足發阿耨多羅三藐三菩提心也。

次勸常持菩提心。

普告大眾。若僧若俗。既已發菩提大心。修菩薩妙道。至誠普啟諸佛。一心普攝眾生。

简体字　　　　　　　　　正體字

In the *Floral Adornment Sutra*'s "Conduct and Vows" chapter, it states, "When a person approaches the end of life, in that very last instant, all of one's faculties scatter into ruination. All of one's relatives and retinue abandon one and leave. All of one's power completely recedes and is lost...." As for all of one's wealth and treasures: "None of them ever again accompany one. It is only these kings of vows which do not forsake one and depart. They always continue to lead one along straight on through..." until one reaches bodhi.... "Therefore you who hear of these kings of vows must not generate doubting thoughts about them."[20]

> **Interlinear note:** This is what is spoken by Samantabhadra at the very end of the *Floral Adornment [Sutra]*. It is certainly not either false or erroneous. One should rely upon this in one's cultivation of the practices.

Explanation of the Five Vows

First, beings are boundlessly many. I vow to liberate them all.
Second, merit and wisdom are boundless. I vow to accumulate them.
Third, the Dharma of the Buddha is boundless. I vow to study it.
Fourth, the Tathāgatas are boundlessly many. I vow to serve them.
Fifth, I vow to realize the unsurpassed, right enlightenment.

One maintains these five vows, implementing them in one's mind in thought after thought such that there is no interval in which they are not active. This constitutes complete implementation of the great mind of bodhi. This is what constitutes the upholding of the precepts of the bodhi mind. The three types of minds and the five vows are layered one upon the other in a way whereby they support each other.

From one buddha to the next, the path is the same. It does not go beyond this. It is precisely this which constitutes perfect generation of the *anuttarasamyaksaṃbodhi* mind.

Exhortation to Constantly Maintain the Bodhi Resolve

Let it be known throughout the Great Community that, whether Sangha or laity, having generated the great resolve determined to realize bodhi and having begun cultivation of the bodhisattva's marvelous path, one then, imbued with utmost sincerity, announces this universally to all buddhas. One proceeds then to single-mindedly engage in universally attracting all beings and,

行住坐卧常持此愿。不欺诳
于六道。不失信于如来。广
设津梁。护持教法。弥勒座
下。皆证无生。千佛会中。
俱为导首。能持此心。则永
不退失阿耨多罗三藐三菩
提。

次劝度脱众生。

普告大众。若僧若俗。从今
身至佛身。誓欲度脱一切众
生。普令入佛知见。黑暗岸
下为作明灯。生死海中为船
筏。力虽未及。常运此心。
念念相续。不令间断。能持
此心否。若持此心。则永不
退失阿耨多罗三藐三菩提。

次劝积集福德。

普告大众。若僧若俗。从今
身至佛身。誓欲于悲田敬田
积集福德。亦舍内财外财成
就万行本。为众生修道须资
福德胜缘。令无私己之心欲
受天人之报。

简体字

行住坐臥常持此願。不欺誑
於六道。不失信於如來。廣
設津梁。護持教法。彌勒座
下。皆證無生。千佛會中。
俱為導首。能持此心。則永
不退失阿耨多羅三藐三菩
提。

次勸度脫眾生。

普告大眾。若僧若俗。從今
身至佛身。誓欲度脫一切眾
生。普令入佛知見。黑闇岸
下為作明燈。生死海中為船
筏。力雖未及。常運此心。
念念相續。不令間斷。能持
此心否。若持此心。則永不
退失阿耨多羅三藐三菩提。

次勸積集福德。

普告大眾。若僧若俗。從今
身至佛身。誓欲於悲田敬田
積集福德。亦捨內財外財成
就萬行本。為眾生修道須資
福德勝緣。令無私己之心欲
受天人之報。

正體字

whether walking, standing, sitting, or lying down, one constantly upholds these vows.

One never lapses into cheating or deceiving those who abide in the six destinies and never fails to uphold the trust of the Tathāgatas. One broadly establishes bridging methods for the protection and maintenance of the instructional Dharma. May it be then that, before Maitreya's [Dharma] throne, we will all be able to realize the unproduced-dharmas patience (*anutpattikadharmakṣānti*). May it be as well that, in the assemblies of the Thousand Buddhas, we will all serve as leaders among their [Dharma] guides.

If one is able to maintain this [bodhi] resolve, then one will never retreat from and thus fail to realize *anuttarasamyaksaṃbodhi*.

Exhortation to Liberate Beings

Let it be known throughout the Great Community that, whether Sangha or laity, we should now vow that from the present life until gaining the buddha body, we shall strive to liberate all beings, causing them all to enter into the knowledge and vision of the Buddhas. We now vow that, along the darkened shores, we will serve as bright lamps, and, out on the sea of cyclic birth-and-death, we will serve as ships and rafts.

Even though our powers have not yet reached this point, nonetheless we shall constantly implement this mind so that it remains continuous in thought-after-thought and is not allowed to be interrupted or cut off. Are you able to maintain this mind, or not? If one is able to maintain this [bodhi] resolve, then one will never retreat from and fail to realize *anuttarasamyaksaṃbodhi*.

Exhortation to Accumulate Merit

Let it be known throughout the Great Community that, whether Sangha or laity, we should now vow that, from the present life on until gaining the buddha body, we shall strive to accumulate merit within the merit-field of compassion and the merit-field of reverence while also relinquishing our inward wealth and outward wealth in perfecting the myriad practices. As it is fundamentally for the sake of beings that we cultivate the Path, it is essential that we avail ourselves of the aid of the superior conditions inherent in this merit. We must not allow a self-serving mind to hold sway whereby we might fall into a desire to take on the karmic rewards of gods or men.

力虽未及。常运此心。念念
相续。不令间断。能持此心
否。若持此心。则永不退失
阿耨多罗三藐三菩提。

次劝修学佛法。

普告大众。若僧若俗。从今
身至佛身。誓欲修一切佛
法。穷一切教门。四无量
心。六波罗蜜。法义深浅。
因果有无。性相二宗。顿渐
二教。悉皆通达。开导众
生。力虽未及。常运此心。
念念相续。不令间断。能持
此心否。若持此心。则永不
退失阿耨多罗三藐三菩提。

次劝亲事诸佛善知识。

普告大众。若僧若俗。从今
身至佛身。誓欲承事诸佛。
一切诸大菩萨。诸善知识。
见善知识情无厌足。事善知
识心无疲懈。闻善知识所有
教诲欣乐顺行。常学善财童
子所行之行。力虽未及。常
运此心。

力雖未及。常運此心。念念
相續。不令間斷。能持此心
否。若持此心。則永不退失
阿耨多羅三藐三菩提。

次勸修學佛法。

普告大眾。若僧若俗。從今
身至佛身。誓欲修一切佛
法。窮一切教門。四無量
心。六波羅蜜。法義深淺。
因果有無。性相二宗。頓漸
二教。悉皆通達。開導眾
生。力雖未及。常運此心。
念念相續。不令間斷。能持
此心否。若持此心。則永不
退失阿耨多羅三藐三菩提。

次勸親事諸佛善知識。

普告大眾。若僧若俗。從今
身至佛身。誓欲承事諸佛。
一切諸大菩薩。諸善知識。
見善知識情無厭足。事善知
識心無疲懈。聞善知識所有
教誨欣樂順行。常學善財童
子所行之行。力雖未及。常
運此心。

简体字 正體字

Even though our powers have not yet reached this point, nonetheless we shall constantly implement this mind so that it remains continuous in thought-after-thought and is not allowed to be interrupted or cut off. Are you able to maintain this mind, or not? If one is able to maintain this [bodhi] resolve, then one will never retreat from and fail to realize *anuttarasamyaksaṃbodhi*.

Exhortation to Cultivate Study of the Buddha's Dharma

Let it be known throughout the Great Community that, whether Sangha or laity, we should now vow that, from the present life on until gaining the buddha body, we shall strive to cultivate all of the dharmas of the Buddhas, exhausting all of the instructional gateways. Thus, in order to instruct and lead forth beings, we shall gain a penetrative understanding of the four immeasurable minds,[21] the six pāramitās,[22] the deep and superficial meanings of Dharma, cause and effect, existence and non-existence, the two doctrinal lineages which focus on the "nature" and "dharmic characteristics," and the two teachings of "sudden" and "gradual" [enlightenment].

Even though our powers have not yet reached this point, nonetheless we shall constantly implement this mind so that it remains continuous in thought-after-thought and is not allowed to be interrupted or cut off. Are you able to maintain this mind, or not? If one is able to maintain this [bodhi] resolve, then one will never retreat from and fail to realize *anuttarasamyaksaṃbodhi*.

Exhortation to Serve Buddhas and Good Spiritual Guides

Let it be known throughout the Great Community that, whether Sangha or laity, we should now vow that, from the present life on until gaining the buddha body, we shall strive to serve the Buddhas, all of the great bodhisattvas, and the good spiritual guides (*kalyāṇa-mitra*).

When we encounter the good spiritual guide, it will be with a disposition of unwearying interest. When we serve the good spiritual guide, it will be with a mind free of fatigue or indolence. When we listen to whatever the good spiritual guide sets forth as teachings, we shall happily accept them and accord with them in our practice, constantly emulating in our study those forms of practice implemented by the splendid youth, Sudhana (*sudhana-śreṣṭhi-dāraka*).[23]

Even though our powers have not yet reached this point, nonetheless we shall constantly implement this mind so that it remains

念念相续。不令间断。能持此心否。若持此心。则永不退失阿耨多罗三藐三菩提。

次劝修唯求佛果。

普告大众。若僧若俗。从今身至佛身。常愿当来作佛。不起二乘之心。愿普与一切众生。同体速成正觉。所修善业。一一回向阿耨多罗三藐三菩提。所劝众生。一一令发无上道意。常修宝海梵志广大悲愿力。虽未及常运此心。念念相续。不令间断。能持此心否。若持此心。则永不退失阿耨多罗三藐三菩提。

次劝结菩提道俗。

普告大众。若僧若俗。从今身至佛身。与同发菩提心道俗。生生世世不相舍离。同愿同心。同行同德。各修定慧。分化众生。或为兄弟。或为师长。迭相劝发。彼此护持。一

念念相續。不令間斷。能持此心否。若持此心。則永不退失阿耨多羅三藐三菩提。

次勸修唯求佛果。

普告大眾。若僧若俗。從今身至佛身。常願當來作佛。不起二乘之心。願普與一切眾生。同體速成正覺。所修善業。一一回向阿耨多羅三藐三菩提。所勸眾生。一一令發無上道意。常修寶海梵志廣大悲願力。雖未及常運此心。念念相續。不令間斷。能持此心否。若持此心。則永不退失阿耨多羅三藐三菩提。

次勸結菩提道俗。

普告大眾。若僧若俗。從今身至佛身。與同發菩提心道俗。生生世世不相捨離。同願同心。同行同德。各修定慧。分化眾生。或為兄弟。或為師長。迭相勸發。彼此護持。一

简体字   正體字

continuous in thought-after-thought and is not allowed to be inter-rupted or cut off. Are you able to maintain this mind, or not? If one is able to maintain this [bodhi] resolve, then one will never retreat from and fail to realize *anuttarasamyaksaṃbodhi*.

Exhortation to Solely Cultivate the Fruit of Buddhahood

Let it be known throughout the Great Community that, whether Sangha or laity, from the present life on until gaining the buddha body, we must always maintain the aspiration that, in the future, we shall become buddhas. We shall not generate an aspiration to seek the Two Vehicles.[24]

We shall maintain the aspiration that, as we are all universally of the same substance with all beings, we must all swiftly gain realization of the right enlightenment. Thus we shall transfer [the merit from] each and every act of wholesome karma which we cul-tivate, dedicating it to *anuttarasamyaksaṃbodhi*. In each and every case, we shall influence those beings whom we encourage towards generation of the intention to realize the unsurpassed path. We shall always cultivate such vast and greatly compassionate vows as exemplified by the Brahmacārin "Jeweled Sea."[25]

Even though our powers have not yet reached this point, none-theless we shall constantly implement this mind so that it remains continuous in thought-after-thought and is not allowed to be inter-rupted or cut off. Are you able to maintain this mind, or not? If one is able to maintain this [bodhi] resolve, then one will never retreat from and fail to realize *anuttarasamyaksaṃbodhi*.

Exhortation to Sustain Ties with Bodhi-Resolved Sangha & Laity

Let it be known throughout the Great Community that, whether Sangha or laity, from the present life on until gaining the buddha body, we shall, in life-after-life, refrain from forsaking and aban-doning monastics and laity who have, just the same as us, gener-ated the resolve to realize bodhi. [For the sake of] those of the same vows, the same resolve, the same practice, and the same merito-rious qualities, we shall each cultivate meditative absorption and wisdom, and shall separately engage in the transformative teaching of beings, in some cases serving as an older or younger brother, and in other cases serving as a mentor or elder.

We shall take turns in providing mutual encouragement and inspiration and in guarding and supporting one another. When

人失路即同拯拔。一人证道即共归依。永无猒倦。不相舍离。能持此心否。若持此心。则永不退失阿耨多罗三藐三菩提。

次劝通圆顿经典。

普告大众。若僧若俗。既已发菩提大心。运菩提大行。若不彻菩提心体。未合菩提法源。虽已发心。必滞摧小。故须先悟圆明净觉。本无无明。幻翳空华。俱非实体。远离执取。平如虚空。常于寂照。心中流出广大大悲智。如此则不滞诸相。不堕二边。始为菩提正因。方免枉受劳苦。若金刚圆觉。简妙通明。华严涅盘。广大具足。傥同我志。并望通经。

次明一切助菩提法。

宝海梵志。劝无量人发

人失路即同拯拔。一人證道即共歸依。永無猒倦。不相捨離。能持此心否。若持此心。則永不退失阿耨多羅三藐三菩提。

次勸通圓頓經典。

普告大眾。若僧若俗。既已發菩提大心。運菩提大行。若不徹菩提心體。未合菩提法源。雖已發心。必滯摧小。故須先悟圓明淨覺。本無無明。幻翳空華。俱非實體。遠離執取。平如虛空。常於寂照。心中流出廣大大悲智。如此則不滯諸相。不墮二邊。始為菩提正因。方免枉受勞苦。若金剛圓覺。簡妙通明。華嚴涅槃。廣大具足。儻同我志。並望通經。

次明一切助菩提法。

寶海梵志。勸無量人發

简体字

正體字

one person loses the Path, we shall work together to rescue him and extricate him from difficulty. When one person gains realization of the Path, we shall immediately take the Refuges with him. We shall remain ever tireless in refraining from forsaking or abandoning one another.

Are you able to maintain this resolve or not? If one is able to maintain this resolve, then one will never retreat from and fail to realize *anuttarasamyaksaṃbodhi*.

Exhortation to Fathom "Perfect-and-Sudden Teaching" Sutras

Let it be known throughout the Great Community that, whether Sangha or laity, although one has already generated the great bodhi resolve and has already taken up the great bodhi-related practices, so long as one has failed to penetratingly fathom the very essence of the bodhi mind, one still fails to unite with the very source of the dharma of bodhi. Thus, although one has already generated the resolve, still, one is certain to stagnate in the provisional[26] and lesser-scope [teachings].[27]

Therefore, it is essential to first gain an awakening whereby one comprehends that the perfect, bright, and pure enlightenment is originally devoid of any delusive ignorance. The illusional obscurations and "flowers floating in space"[28] do not constitute the substance of reality. [This enlightened mind] is distantly separate from any sort of attachment-based grasping and is as uniform in nature as empty space itself. Expansively great compassion and wisdom constantly flow forth from this quiescent and radiant mind.[29]

When one accords with this, then [one's mind] no longer stagnates in phenomenal characteristics and no longer falls into the two extremes.[30] It is at this point that one first develops the correct cause of bodhi. Only then is one able to avoid wrongly undergoing toilsome suffering. [Scriptures] such as the *Vajra [Prajñāpāramitā]* and the *Perfect Enlightenment* are brief and sublimely marvelous [while also communicating] penetrating comprehension. The *Floral Adornment* and *Nirvāṇa* are vast, grand, and complete in their perfection. Where[31] there are those who harbor the same aspiration as I do, we might all aspire to fathom these scriptures.

Explanation of all Bodhi-Assisting Dharmas

[In the *Flower of Compassion Sutra*[32]], the Brahmacārin "Jeweled Sea" encouraged an incalculable number of people to generate the

阿耨多罗三藐三菩提心。取
佛世界皆得受记。复劝三亿
弟子令其发心。中有一人名
曰树提。白言。尊者云何菩
提。云何助菩提法。云何菩
萨修行菩提。云何系念得于
菩提。尔时。其师报言。菩
提者。即是菩萨之所修集四
无量藏。所谓无尽福德藏。
无尽智藏。无尽慧藏。无尽
佛法和合藏。是名菩提。如
佛所说助菩提法。所谓摄取
清净度生死法门。善男子舍
财是助菩提法。调伏众生。
故持戒是助菩提法。随其所
愿得成就。故忍辱是助菩提
法。三十二相八十随形好具
足。故精进是助菩提法。具
足一切诸事。故禅定是助菩
提法。其心当得善调伏。故
智慧是助菩提法。知一切诸
烦恼。故多闻是助菩提法。
得无碍辨。故福德是助菩提
法。一切众生之所须。故思
惟是助菩提法。成就断疑。
故

阿耨多羅三藐三菩提心。取
佛世界皆得受記。復勸三億
弟子令其發心。中有一人名
曰樹提。白言。尊者云何菩
提。云何助菩提法。云何菩
薩修行菩提。云何繫念得於
菩提。爾時。其師報言。菩
提者。即是菩薩之所修集四
無量藏。所謂無盡福德藏。
無盡智藏。無盡慧藏。無盡
佛法和合藏。是名菩提。如
佛所說助菩提法。所謂攝取
清淨度生死法門。善男子捨
財是助菩提法。調伏眾生。
故持戒是助菩提法。隨其所
願得成就。故忍辱是助菩提
法。三十二相八十隨形好具
足。故精進是助菩提法。具
足一切諸事。故禪定是助菩
提法。其心當得善調伏。故
智慧是助菩提法。知一切諸
煩惱。故多聞是助菩提法。
得無礙辨。故福德是助菩提
法。一切眾生之所須。故思
惟是助菩提法。成就斷疑。
故

简体字　　　　　　　　　　　　　　正體字

anuttarasamyaksaṃbodhi resolve and to select buddhalands where they all succeeded in receiving predictions of future buddhahood.

He additionally encouraged three *koṭīs* of disciples, influencing them to generate the [bodhi] resolve. Among them was a man named Shu-ti[33] who addressed him, saying, "Venerable one. What is meant by 'bodhi'? What are the dharmas which assist bodhi? How is it that a bodhisattva goes about cultivating bodhi? How is it that, through focusing one's mindfulness, one realizes bodhi?"

His guru replied to him, saying, "As for 'bodhi,' it is precisely those four inexhaustible[34] treasuries which are cultivated and accumulated by the bodhisattva, namely the treasury of inexhaustible merit, the treasury of inexhaustible knowledges, the treasury of inexhaustible wisdom, and the treasury of the inexhaustible unified Dharma of the Buddha. It is these things which serve to constitute what we term 'bodhi.'

"According to the Buddha's explanation of what constitutes the bodhi-assisting dharmas, they consist in the accumulation of pure Dharma gateways through which one achieves liberation from cyclic birth-and-death.

"Son of Good Family, the relinquishing of one's wealth is a bodhi-assisting dharma because, on account of it, one succeeds in the restraint and training of beings.[35]

"Upholding the moral prohibitions is a bodhi-assisting dharma because, on account of it, no matter what a person aspires to, it results in success.

"Patience is a bodhi-assisting dharma because, on account of it, one perfects the thirty-two physical marks and the eighty subsidiary characteristics.

"Vigor is a bodhi-assisting dharma because, on account of it, one succeeds in the perfect accomplishment of all endeavors.

"Dhyāna absorption is a bodhi-assisting dharma because, on account of it, one's mind is skillfully subdued and trained.

"Wisdom is a bodhi-assisting dharma because, on account of it, one becomes aware of all forms of afflictions.

"Extensive learning is a bodhi-assisting dharma because, on account of it, one gains unimpeded eloquence.

"[The accumulation of] merit is a bodhi-assisting dharma because it is an essential necessity for all beings.

"Contemplative reflection is a bodhi-assisting dharma because, on account of it, one succeeds in severing doubts.

慈心是助菩提法。成就无碍
心。故悲心是助菩提法。教
化众生无厌足。故喜心是助
菩提法。于正法中生爱乐。
故舍心是助菩提法。成就断
于爱憎。故听法是助菩提
法。成就灭五盖。故出世是
助菩提法。舍除一切世间。
故阿兰若是助菩提法。灭不
善业。故随喜是助菩提法。
增长善根。故念处是助菩提
法。分别身受心法成就。故
正勤是助菩提法。离一切不
善法行一切善法。故如意足
是助菩提法。成就身心轻
利。故诸根是助菩提法。摧
灭一切烦恼。故觉是助菩提
法。觉如实法。故

慈心是助菩提法。成就無礙
心。故悲心是助菩提法。教
化眾生無厭足。故喜心是助
菩提法。於正法中生愛樂。
故捨心是助菩提法。成就斷
於愛憎。故聽法是助菩提
法。成就滅五蓋。故出世是
助菩提法。捨除一切世間。
故阿蘭若是助菩提法。滅不
善業。故隨喜是助菩提法。
增長善根。故念處是助菩提
法。分別身受心法成就。故
正勤是助菩提法。離一切不
善法行一切善法。故如意足
是助菩提法。成就身心輕
利。故諸根是助菩提法。摧
滅一切煩惱。故覺是助菩提
法。覺如實法。故

简体字 正體字

"The mind imbued with loving-kindness is a bodhi-assisting dharma because, on account of it, one perfects a mind free of obstructiveness.

"The compassionate mind is a bodhi-assisting dharma because, on account of it, one carries on tirelessly with the teaching and transforming of beings.

"The mind suffused with sympathetic joy is a bodhi-assisting dharma because, on account of it, one is able to bring forth affectionate happiness based on right Dharma.

"The mind of equanimity is a bodhi-assisting dharma because, on account of it, one succeeds in severing both affection and loathing.

"Listening to Dharma is a bodhi-assisting dharma because, on account of it, one is able to succeed in putting an end to the five hindrances (lit. "coverings").[36]

"Transcending the world is a bodhi-assisting dharma because, on account of it, one is able to renounce and abandon all aspects of worldly existence.

"Dwelling in an *araṇya*[37] is a bodhi-assisting dharma because, on account of it, one is able to destroy unwholesome karmic activity.

"Joyfully according [with the wholesome karmic actions of others] is a bodhi-assisting dharma because, on account of it, one is able to bring about the growth of one's roots of goodness.

"The [four] stations of mindfulness are bodhi-assisting dharmas because, on account of them, one is able to perfect one's analytic comprehension of the body, feelings, thoughts, and dharmas (i.e. "phenomena").[38]

"The [four] right efforts are bodhi-assisting dharmas because, on account of them, one is able to abandon all unwholesome dharmas and carry on with the practice of all good dharmas.[39]

"The [four] bases of psychic power are bodhi-assisting dharmas because, on account of them, one is able to perfect the light easefulness (*praśrabdhi*) of both body and mind.[40]

"The [five] 'root-faculties' are bodhi-assisting dharmas [because, on account of them, one consolidates the faculties.[41]

"The {five} powers are bodhi-assisting dharmas] because, on account of them, one destroys all afflictions.[42]

"The [seven] limbs of enlightenment are bodhi-assisting dharmas because, on account of them, one becomes enlightened to an awareness of dharmas which accords with ultimate reality.[43]

六和是助菩提法。调伏众生
令清净。故是名摄取清净度
生死法门。如是修行。即系
念得菩提也。 如是等菩提
心。今应生欲。是道清净。
是道无漏。是道正直。是道
安稳。汝等应当专心作大誓
愿。取庄严佛土。随意所
求。

（庄严佛土各各不同也。或
取净土或取秽土。具在悲华
经中。）

次明菩萨四懈怠法。

宝藏如来告毗舍那无垢言。
菩萨有四懈怠。若菩萨成就
四法。于生死狱。受诸苦
恼。不能疾成阿耨多罗三藐
三菩提。何等为四。所谓下
行。下伴。下施。下愿。云
何下行。或有菩萨破口身戒
不善护业。是名下行。云何
下伴。亲近声闻及辟支佛共
与同事。是名下伴。云何下
施。不能一切舍诸所有。于
受者中心生分别。

六和是助菩提法。調伏眾生
令清淨。故是名攝取清淨度
生死法門。如是修行。即繫
念得菩提也。 如是等菩提
心。今應生欲。是道清淨。
是道無漏。是道正直。是道
安穩。汝等應當專心作大誓
願。取莊嚴佛土。隨意所
求。

（莊嚴佛土各各不同也。或
取淨土或取穢土。具在悲華
經中。）

次明菩薩四懈怠法。

寶藏如來告毗舍那無垢言。
菩薩有四懈怠。若菩薩成就
四法。於生死獄。受諸苦
惱。不能疾成阿耨多羅三藐
三菩提。何等為四。所謂下
行。下伴。下施。下願。云
何下行。或有菩薩破口身戒
不善護業。是名下行。云何
下伴。親近聲聞及辟支佛共
與同事。是名下伴。云何下
施。不能一切捨諸所有。於
受者中心生分別。

简体字　　　　　　　　　　正體字

"The six harmonies are bodhi-assisting dharmas because, on account of them, one is able to restrain and train beings while influencing them towards purification.[44]

"...These [sorts of practices] are what qualify as 'the accumulation of pure Dharma gateways through which one brings about liberation from cyclic birth-and-death.'

"...To cultivate in this manner is in itself precisely what is meant by realizing bodhi through focusing of one's mindfulness.

"...Such manifestations of the bodhi mind as these are those towards which one should now generate zeal. This path is pure. ... This path is free of outflow impurities. ...This path is correct and direct. ... This path[45] is peaceful and secure. ...You all should, with focused minds, make great vows whereby you choose to take up the adornment of whichever sorts of buddhalands accord with your respective aspirations."

> **Interlinear note:** In this matter of the adornment of buddhalands, each individual is different. Some will select a pure land. Some will select a defiled land. This is described in full in the *Flower of Compassion Sutra.*

Explanation of the Four Bodhisattva Indolence Dharmas

Jeweled Treasury Tathāgata spoke to Vijaya, the Stainless One,[46] saying, "Among bodhisattvas, there exist four indolence-associated dharmas. If the bodhisattva completely engenders these four dharmas, then he undergoes all manner of suffering and affliction within the prison of cyclic birth-and-death and thus remains unable to swiftly gain realization of *anuttarasamyaksaṃbodhi.*

What then are these four? They are the so-called inferior conduct, inferior companions, inferior giving, and inferior vows.

"What is meant by 'inferior conduct'? There may be times when a bodhisattva breaks moral prohibitions related to verbal and physical karma. Thus he fails then to skillfully guard the quality of his karmic actions. This is what is meant by 'inferior conduct.'

"What is meant by 'inferior companions'? When one draws close to those who adhere to the Śrāvaka (Hearer-disciple) and Pratyekabuddha [vehicles] and then becomes involved with them in taking up the same sorts of endeavors, these then qualify as 'inferior companions'?

"What is meant by 'inferior giving'? When one is unable to relinquish absolutely everything which one possesses, when one

为得天上快乐。故而行布施。是名下施。云何下愿。不能一心愿取诸佛净妙世界。所作誓愿不能调伏众生。是名下愿。（出慈华经。）

次明菩萨四速疾法。

复有四法。菩萨成就。则能疾成阿耨多罗三藐三菩提。一者能持禁戒净。身口意护舍法门行。二者亲近修学大乘之人。与共同事。三者所有之物能一切舍。以大悲心施于一切。四者一心愿取种种庄严诸佛世界。亦为调伏一切众生。是名四法。（出悲华经。）

次明发菩提心功德。

天帝释白法慧菩萨言。佛子菩萨初发菩提心所得功德其量几何。法慧菩萨言。此义甚深。难说。难知。难分别。难信解。难证。难行。难

為得天上快樂。故而行布施。是名下施。云何下願。不能一心願取諸佛淨妙世界。所作誓願不能調伏眾生。是名下願。（出慈華經。）

次明菩薩四速疾法。

復有四法。菩薩成就。則能疾成阿耨多羅三藐三菩提。一者能持禁戒淨。身口意護捨法門行。二者親近修學大乘之人。與共同事。三者所有之物能一切捨。以大悲心施於一切。四者一心願取種種莊嚴諸佛世界。亦為調伏一切眾生。是名四法。（出悲華經。）

次明發菩提心功德。

天帝釋白法慧菩薩言。佛子菩薩初發菩提心所得功德其量幾何。法慧菩薩言。此義甚深。難說。難知。難分別。難信解。難證。難行。難

简体字　　　　　　正體字

generates mental discriminations with regard to the recipient, and when one practices giving for the sake of gaining the bliss of celestial existences, this is what qualifies as 'inferior giving.'

"What is meant by 'inferior vows'? When one is unable to single-mindedly vow to choose to go to the pure and marvelous lands of the Buddhas and when the vows one makes are not able to bring about the training and subduing of beings, these qualify as 'inferior vows.'"[47]

Interlinear note: This is from the *Flower of Compassion Sutra*.[48]

Explanation of the Four Bodhisattva Swiftness Dharmas

"...There are yet another four dharmas which, if completely engendered by the bodhisattva, bring about swift realization of *anuttara-samyaksaṃbodhi*.[49]

As for the first, one is able to uphold the restrictive prohibitions, purify body, mouth, and mind, and thus guard and maintain practice of the Dharma gateways.[50]

"As for the second, one draws close to persons who cultivate and study the Great Vehicle and then becomes involved with them in taking up the same sorts of endeavors.

"As for the third, one is able to relinquish everything one possesses and employ the greatly compassionate mind to engage in giving to everyone.

"As for the fourth, one single-mindedly vows to choose to go to and adorn in many different ways the lands of the Buddhas while also doing so for the sake of training and subduing all beings.

"These are what constitute the four [bodhisattva swiftness] dharmas."

Interlinear note: This is from the *Flower of Compassion Sutra*.

Description of the Merit from Generating the Bodhi Resolve

[**Translator's Note:** This entire section is extracted from the *Floral Adornment (Avataṃsaka) Sutra*.[51]]

[At that time], the God, Śakra Devānām Indra inquired of Dharma Wisdom Bodhisattva, saying, "Son of the Buddha, how much merit is gained by the bodhisattva when he first generates the bodhi resolve?"

Dharma Wisdom Bodhisattva replied, saying, "The meaning of this is extremely profound, difficult to describe, difficult to know, difficult to analyze, difficult to believe and comprehend, difficult

通达。难思惟。难度量。难趣入。虽然我当承佛威神之力而为汝说。佛子。假使有人以一切乐具供养东方阿僧只世界所有众生。经于一劫。然后教令净持五戒。南西北方四维上下亦复如是。此人功德宁为多否。天帝言。此人功德唯佛能知。法慧言。此人功德比菩萨初发心功德。百分不及一。千分不及一。百千分不及一。如是亿分。百亿分。千亿分。百千亿分。那由他亿分。百那由他亿分。千那由他亿分。百千那由他亿分。百万那由他亿分。乃至优波尼沙陀亿分。亦不及一。佛子且置此喻。假使有人以一切乐具供养十方阿僧只世界所有众生。经于百劫。然后教令修十善道。如是供养。经于千劫教住四禅。经百千劫教住四无量心。经于亿劫教住四无色定。经百亿

通達。難思惟。難度量。難趣入。雖然我當承佛威神之力而為汝說。佛子。假使有人以一切樂具供養東方阿僧祇世界所有眾生。經於一劫。然後教令淨持五戒。南西北方四維上下亦復如是。此人功德寧為多否。天帝言。此人功德唯佛能知。法慧言。此人功德比菩薩初發心功德。百分不及一。千分不及一。百千分不及一。如是億分。百億分。千億分。百千億分。那由他億分。百那由他億分。千那由他億分。百千那由他億分。百萬那由他億分。乃至優波尼沙陀億分。亦不及一。佛子且置此喻。假使有人以一切樂具供養十方阿僧祇世界所有眾生。經於百劫。然後教令修十善道。如是供養。經於千劫教住四禪。經百千劫教住四無量心。經於億劫教住四無色定。經百億

简体字   正體字

to achieve the realization of, difficult to bring into action, difficult to penetratingly understand, difficult to contemplate, difficult to calculate, and difficult to proceed into. Although this is the case, I shall nonetheless endeavor, through the support of the Buddha's awesome spiritual powers, to explain this matter for you.

"Son of the Buddha. If there were a person who took up every form of happiness-providing phenomena and made offerings of them to all of the beings off in the eastern direction in a number of worlds amounting to an *asaṃkhyeya*'s quantity, and continued to do this for an entire kalpa, and then afterwards instructed them and influenced them to uphold the five precepts purely—and if he also performed the same actions in the same way in all of the other directions of the south, west, north, the four midpoints, the zenith, and the nadir—would that person's merit be abundant, or not?"

Śakra Devānām Indra replied, "Only the Buddha would be able to know the extent of this person's merit."

Dharma Wisdom continued, "This person's merit, when compared to the merit of the bodhisattva who has initially generated the bodhi resolve, does not amount to even a hundredth part, does not amount to a thousandth part, does not amount to a hundred-thousandth part. Similarly, it does not amount to one part in a *koṭī*, does not amount to one part in a hundred *koṭīs*, to one part in one thousand *koṭīs*, to one part in one hundred thousand *koṭīs*, to one part in a *nayuta* of *koṭīs*, to one part in a hundred *nayutas* of *koṭīs*, to one part in a thousand *nayutas* of *koṭīs*, to one part in a hundred thousand *nayutas* of *koṭīs*, to one part in a million *nayutas* of *koṭīs*..." and so forth until we come to "not amounting to even a single *upaniṣad*'s fraction.[52]

"Son of the Buddha. Moreover, one may simply set aside this analogy. If instead there were a person who utilized all forms of happiness-providing phenomena to make offerings to all of the beings in an *asaṃkhyeya*[53] of worlds in each of the ten directions and did so for a hundred kalpas and then afterwards instructed them in a manner causing them to cultivate the path of the ten wholesome karmic actions,[54] performing this sort of offering for a thousand kalpas—and if he then taught beings and caused them to abide in the four dhyānas, doing so for a period of a hundred thousand kalpas—and if he then taught beings and caused them to abide in the four limitless minds, doing so for a period of a *koṭī* of kalpas—and if he then instructed beings and caused them to abide

劫教住须陀洹果。经于千亿劫教住斯陀含果。经于百千亿劫教住阿那含果。经于那由他亿劫教住阿罗汉果。经于百千那由他亿劫教住辟支佛道。是人功德宁为多否。天帝言。此人功德唯佛能知。法慧菩萨言。此人功德比菩萨初发心功德百分不及一。乃至优婆尼沙陀分亦不及一。何以故。一切诸佛初发心时。不但为以一切乐具供养十方十阿僧只世界所有众生。经于百劫。乃至百千那由他亿劫故。发菩提心不但为教尔所众生。令修五戒。十善业道。教住四禅。四无量。四无色定。教得须陀洹果。斯陀含果.阿那含果。阿罗汉果。辟支佛道故。发菩提心为令如来种性不断故。为充遍一切世界故。为度脱一切世界众生故。为悉知一切世界成坏故。为悉知一切世界中众生垢净故。

劫教住須陀洹果。經於千億劫教住斯陀含果。經於百千億劫教住阿那含果。經於那由他億劫教住阿羅漢果。經於百千那由他億劫教住辟支佛道。是人功德寧為多否。天帝言。此人功德唯佛能知。法慧菩薩言。此人功德比菩薩初發心功德百分不及一。乃至優婆尼沙陀分亦不及一。何以故。一切諸佛初發心時。不但為以一切樂具供養十方十阿僧祇世界所有眾生。經於百劫。乃至百千那由他億劫故。發菩提心不但為教爾所眾生。令修五戒。十善業道。教住四禪。四無量。四無色定。教得須陀洹果。斯陀含果.阿那含果。阿羅漢果。辟支佛道故。發菩提心為令如來種性不斷故。為充遍一切世界故。為度脫一切世界眾生故。為悉知一切世界成壞故。為悉知一切世界中眾生垢淨故。

简体字　　　　　　　　　正體字

in the four formless absorptions, doing so for a period of a hundred *koṭīs* of kalpas—and if he then instructed beings, causing them to abide in the fruit of the *srota-āpanna*,[55] doing so for a period of a thousand *koṭīs* of kalpas—and if he then instructed beings, causing them to abide in the fruit of the *sakṛdāgāmin*,[56] doing so for a period of a hundred-thousand *koṭīs* of kalpas—and if he then instructed beings, causing them to abide in the fruit of the *ānāgamin*,[57] doing so for a period of a *nayuta* of *koṭīs* of kalpas—and if he then instructed beings, causing them to abide in the fruit of the arhat, doing so for a period of a hundred-thousand *nayutas* of *koṭīs* of kalpas—and if he then instructed beings, influencing them to abide in the path of a pratyekabuddha—would this persons's merit be abundant, or not?"

Śakra Devānām Indra replied, "Only the Buddha would be able to know the extent of this person's merit."

Dharma Wisdom Bodhisattva then said, "This person's merit, when compared to the merit of the bodhisattva who has initially generated the bodhi resolve, does not amount to even a hundredth part and so forth until we come to does not even amount to an *upaniṣad's* fraction. Why is this the case?

"When all Buddhas first generate the [bodhi] resolve, they do not generate the bodhi resolve solely for the sake of utilizing all forms of happiness-providing phenomena in the making of offerings to all beings in ten *asaṃkhyeyas* of worlds in the ten directions for a period of one hundred kalpas, and so forth until we come to a hundred-thousand *nayutas* of *koṭīs* of kalpas.

"Nor do they generate the bodhi resolve solely for the sake of teaching so many beings and thus influencing them to cultivate the five precepts or the path of the ten wholesome karmic deeds, or for the sake of teaching them to abide in the four dhyānas, in the four immeasurables, in the four formless absorptions, or for the sake of teaching them to gain the fruit of the *srota-āpanna*, the fruit of the *sakṛdāgāmin*, the fruit of the *ānāgamin*, the fruit of the arhat, or the path-[result] of a pratyekabuddha.

"When they generate the unsurpassed bodhi resolve, it is for the sake of preventing the lineage of the Tathāgatas from being cut off. It is for the sake of their being able to fill up and pervade all worlds [with the influence of Dharma]. It is for the sake of liberating the beings in all worlds. It is for the sake of utterly knowing the creation and destruction of all worlds. It is for the sake of utterly knowing the defilement and purity of the beings in all worlds. It is

为悉知一切世界自性清净故。为悉知一切众生心乐烦恼习气故。为悉知一切众生死此生彼故。为悉知一切众生诸根方便故。为悉知一切众生心行故。为悉知一切众生三世智故。为悉知一切佛境界平等故。发于无上菩提之心故。常为三世一切诸佛之所忆念。当得三世一切诸佛与其妙法。即与三世一切诸佛体性平等。已修三世一切诸佛助道之法。成就三世一切诸佛力无所畏。庄严三世一切诸佛不共佛法。悉得法界一切诸佛说法智慧。何以故。以是发心。当得佛故。应知此人即与三世诸佛同等。即与三世诸佛境界平等。即与三世诸佛功德平等。得如来一身无量身究竟平等真实智慧。初发心时。即为十方一切诸佛所共称叹。即能说法教化。调伏一切世界所有众生。即能震动一切世界。即能光照一切

為悉知一切世界自性清淨故。為悉知一切眾生心樂煩惱習氣故。為悉知一切眾生死此生彼故。為悉知一切眾生諸根方便故。為悉知一切眾生心行故。為悉知一切眾生三世智故。為悉知一切佛境界平等故。發於無上菩提之心故。常為三世一切諸佛之所憶念。當得三世一切諸佛與其妙法。即與三世一切諸佛體性平等。已修三世一切諸佛助道之法。成就三世一切諸佛力無所畏。莊嚴三世一切諸佛不共佛法。悉得法界一切諸佛說法智慧。何以故。以是發心。當得佛故。應知此人即與三世諸佛同等。即與三世諸佛境界平等。即與三世諸佛功德平等。得如來一身無量身究竟平等真實智慧。初發心時。即為十方一切諸佛所共稱歎。即能說法教化。調伏一切世界所有眾生。即能震動一切世界。即能光照一切

for the sake of utterly knowing the purity of the inherent nature of all worlds. It is for the sake of utterly knowing the pleasures, afflictions, and habitual propensities of the minds of all beings. It is for the sake of utterly knowing in regard to all beings their meeting death in this place and their arising to birth in that place. It is for the sake of utterly knowing with regard to all beings their faculties and the appropriate corresponding skillful means. It is for the sake of utterly knowing with regard to all beings the activity occurring in their minds. It is for the sake of utterly knowing with regard to all beings the knowledges relating to the three periods of time. And it is for the sake of utterly knowing the uniformity inhering in the mind state of all buddhas.

"On account of this, [when one initially generates the bodhi resolve] he is constantly borne in mind by all buddhas of the three periods of time and becomes bound to receive bestowal of the marvelous Dharma by all buddhas of the three periods of time. He forthwith becomes uniformly the same in substance and nature with all buddhas of the three periods of time. He has [in effect] already cultivated the path-assisting dharmas of all buddhas of the three periods of time, has already perfected the powers and fearlessnesses of all buddhas of the three periods of time, has already created the adornment of those buddha dharmas exclusive to buddhas possessed by all buddhas of the three periods of time, and has already [in effect] gained in its entirety the Dharma-proclaiming wisdom of all buddhas throughout the Dharma realm.

"How is this the case? It is on account of this generation of the [bodhi] resolve that one becomes bound to gain the realization of buddhahood. Therefore one should realize that this person immediately becomes identical and equal with all buddhas of the three periods of time, immediately becomes uniformly equal to the mind state of all buddhas of the three periods of time, immediately becomes uniformly equal in merit with all buddhas of the three periods of time, [in effect] gains ultimate identity with the one body and incalculably many bodies of the Tathāgatas, and [in effect gains] their genuine wisdom.

"At that very time of initially generating the [bodhi] resolve, one is immediately praised by all buddhas of the ten directions, immediately becomes able to teach, transform, and subdue all of the beings in all worlds, immediately becomes able to cause the shaking and moving of all worlds, immediately becomes able to

世界。即能息灭一切世界诸
恶道苦。即能严净一切世
界。即能于一切世界中示现
成佛。即能令一切众生皆得
欢喜心。即能入一切法界
性。即能持一切佛种性。即
能得一切佛智慧光明。此初
发心菩萨不于三世少有所
得。若诸佛。若诸佛法。若
诸菩萨。若诸菩萨法。若独
觉。若独觉法。若声闻。若
声闻法。若出世间。若出世
间法。若众生。若众生法。
唯求一切智于诸法界心无所
着。是名初发阿耨多罗三藐
三菩提心功德。

（出华严经发心功德品。此
约初住菩萨说。今凡夫位中
是初发菩提心。至初住位中
是成就菩提心也。）

次通凡圣差别疑。

或曰。菩提大心。圣贤境
界。固非凡夫浅识所能造拟
也。故菩萨初住。

简体字

illuminate all worlds, immediately becomes able to extinguish the suffering in all of the wretched destinies in all worlds, immediately becomes able to adorn and purify all worlds, immediately becomes able to manifest the achievement of buddhahood in all worlds, immediately becomes able to cause delight in the minds of all beings, immediately becomes able to enter into the very nature of the entire Dharma realm, immediately becomes able to maintain the lineage of all buddhas, and immediately becomes able to gain the wisdom light of all buddhas.

"Yet this bodhisattva who has initially generated the [bodhi] resolve does not find that there is even the slightest thing that is attainable in any of the three periods of time, whether that be any of the Buddhas, whether that be any of the Buddhas' dharmas, whether that be any of the Bodhisattvas, whether that be any of the Bodhisattvas' dharmas, whether that be any of the Pratyekabuddhas, whether that be any of the Pratyekabuddhas' dharmas, whether that be any of the Śrāvakas, whether that be any of the Śrāvakas' dharmas, whether that be transcendence of the world, whether that be any of the world-transcending dharmas, whether that be any being, or whether that be any of the dharmas associated with any beings. One solely seeks omniscience. The mind remains free from any attachments whatsoever with respect to any aspect of the Dharma realm."

This is what is involved in the merit associated with the initial generation of the resolve to realize *anuttarasamyaksaṃbodhi*.

> **Interlinear note:** This is extracted from "The Merit Associated with Generating the [Bodhi] Resolve" chapter of the *Floral Adornment [Avataṃsaka] Sutra*. This is an explanation referring to the situation of the bodhisattva abiding in the station known as the first ground.
>
> Now, while abiding in the position of a common person, this is [but the very] initial level of generating the bodhi resolve. Once one [finally] reaches this station of the first ground, one succeeds in perfecting [one's generation of] the bodhi resolve.[58]

Resolving Doubts About Common Persons Versus Āryas

One might [raise a challenge at this point and] say: "But the great bodhi resolve is a mental state exclusively the province of the Āryas and Worthies. It is most certainly *not* something a common person's superficial consciousness might be able to succeed in emulating.

发大心。便能游历十方。广
作佛事。今以大法劝诸凡
夫。无乃根器不同乎。对
曰。不然凡圣同源本无差
别。一念迷倒自取沈沦。若
悟性本圆明。便与诸佛平
等。性上起菩提心。以此修
行即为菩萨。

（菩萨者大心众生也。）

何苦自薄而谓凡夫隔绝哉。
且凡夫位中三毒为本。今既
誓舍财宝以化众生。虽未尽
行自然少贪。誓行四摄以化
众生。虽未尽行自然少瞋。
誓修定慧以度众生。虽未尽
证自然少痴。三法在心便成
法器。所以菩萨不断烦恼唯
兴大悲威德。法门诚不虚
设。又何疑而不为哉。且凡
夫发心是初发菩提心也。初
住发心是成就菩提

發大心。便能遊歷十方。廣
作佛事。今以大法勸諸凡
夫。無乃根器不同乎。對
曰。不然凡聖同源本無差
別。一念迷倒自取沈淪。若
悟性本圓明。便與諸佛平
等。性上起菩提心。以此修
行即為菩薩。

（菩薩者大心眾生也。）

何苦自薄而謂凡夫隔絕哉。
且凡夫位中三毒為本。今既
誓捨財寶以化眾生。雖未盡
行自然少貪。誓行四攝以化
眾生。雖未盡行自然少瞋。
誓修定慧以度眾生。雖未盡
證自然少癡。三法在心便成
法器。所以菩薩不斷煩惱唯
興大悲威德。法門誠不虛
設。又何疑而不為哉。且凡
夫發心是初發菩提心也。初
住發心是成就菩提

简体字　　　　　　　　　　　　　正體字

Thus the bodhisattva abiding at the station of the first ground generates the great mind and then becomes able to roam the ten directions carrying out the work of the Buddhas on a vast scale. Now, however, you are seeking to employ this grand dharma to encourage common persons. Is it not the case, though, that there is really no resolving the problem of their possessing such incomparable [and hence inadequate] faculties and potentials?"

My response to this is to point out that, no, this is *not* the case. The common person and the Āryas share the same source. At root, there are no distinctions. It is simply a matter of a single thought of delusion and inverted views that precipitates one's choosing to sink away into oblivion. If one but awakens to the nature's original perfect brilliance, then one becomes able to generate the bodhi resolve from within the uniformly equal nature of the Buddhas. When one avails oneself of this in one's cultivation one straightaway becomes a bodhisattva.

Interlinear note: Bodhisattvas are beings possessing a great mind.

What's the point of subjecting oneself to self-rebuke while claiming that the common person is cut off [from this endeavor]?

Furthermore, in the station of the common person, the three poisons form one's very basis. Now, having vowed to relinquish one's wealth and treasures to transform beings, although one is not yet able to exhaustively carry out the practice, still, [in carrying this out], one naturally diminishes the extent of one's covetousness.

One also vows to practice the four means of attraction in order to transform beings. Although one is not yet able to exhaustively carry out the practice, still, [in carrying this out], one naturally diminishes the extent of one's animosity. One also vows to cultivate meditative absorption and wisdom in order to liberate beings. Although one is not yet able to exhaustively perfect these realizations, still, [in carrying this out], one naturally diminishes one's delusions.

With the development of these three dharmas in one's mind, one becomes a Dharma vessel. Hence, although the bodhisattva hasn't yet severed the afflictions, if he is merely able to let flourish that awesomely meritorious Dharma gateway of the great compassion, truly, this is not an endeavor commenced in vain. Moreover, how can one be so seized by doubt that one fails to proceed with this?

Furthermore, when the common person generates the [bodhi] resolve, this is but the initial generation of the bodhi resolve. When an individual at the station of the first ground generates the [bodhi]

心也。若待初住方发此心。
初住之前当修何法。除此菩
提正路。尽为生死因缘。但
至轮回何由证入。故释迦如
来从初发心。即于无量生中
事无量诸佛一切佛。所发菩
提心直至然灯佛前方受远
记。宝藏佛会始号大悲。固
须千百生中方得成就。所以
劝诸道俗学我本师世尊。无
以才辨教门。便为甚深法藏
粗识心性。定言无上菩提须
度一切众生。须求一切种
智。贤劫千佛皆种善根。自
然福智弘深。永作世间道
首。普愿大众以此文示此郡
及他州。与我有缘者见此文
当发菩提心。欲发心时。请
先随力舍财物。

心也。若待初住方發此心。
初住之前當修何法。除此菩
提正路。盡為生死因緣。但
至輪回何由證入。故釋迦如
來從初發心。即於無量生中
事無量諸佛一切佛。所發菩
提心直至然燈佛前方受遠
記。寶藏佛會始號大悲。固
須千百生中方得成就。所以
勸諸道俗學我本師世尊。無
以纔辨教門。便為甚深法藏
粗識心性。定言無上菩提須
度一切眾生。須求一切種
智。賢劫千佛皆種善根。自
然福智弘深。永作世間道
首。普願大眾以此文示此郡
及他州。與我有緣者見此文
當發菩提心。欲發心時。請
先隨力捨財物。

简体字

正體字

resolve, this constitutes the perfection of that generation of the bodhi resolve. If one were to wait until reaching the station of the first ground and only then generate this [bodhi] resolve, then just what might it be that one should be cultivating prior to arriving at the station of the first ground?

With the sole exception of this correct path of bodhi, absolutely everything else constitutes causes and conditions for cyclic birth-and-death which only conduce to [entrapment in] cyclic existence. Based on what, then, would you have a person gain realizations and entry [into the bodhisattva path]?

Thus it was that, from the very first time that Shākyamuni Tathāgata generated the [bodhi] resolve, he proceeded thereafter on through countless lifetimes to serve an incalculable number of buddhas. In the location of each of those buddhas, he generated the bodhi resolve, proceeding directly along in this fashion until he arrived in the presence of Burning Lamp Buddha. Only then did he receive the far-off prediction [of buddhahood]. It was in the assembly surrounding Jeweled Treasury Buddha that he was first given the name "Great Compassion."

Certainly one requires a hundred thousand lifetimes before it becomes perfected. And so it is therefore that I encourage all monastics and laity to emulate in their studies our original guru, the Bhagavān.

One should not take the debating of the teaching's tenets to be some recondite Dharma treasury, resorting then to inherently coarse levels of awareness in trumpeting absolute claims about unsurpassed bodhi.

[Concluding Exhortation]

It is essential to liberate all beings. It is essential to strive to gain the knowledge of all modes (*sarva-ākāra-jñatā*) and plant roots of goodness throughout the Auspicious Kalpa during the reigns of the Thousand Buddhas. Thus one's merit and wisdom will naturally become vast and deep such that, in the world, one will always be among the leaders of those who serve as guides [on the Path].

I pray that all in the Great Community may be able to utilize this text in providing instruction both within this jurisdiction and beyond, in other districts. May those who have affinities with me generate the bodhi resolve on merely perusing this essay.

When about to [formally] generate the [bodhi] resolve, it is

简体字	正體字
或投一斋供养三宝。或画一像精进道场。然后依此正文。虔发大愿。	或投一齋供養三寶。或畫一像精進道場。然後依此正文。虔發大願。
（准贤劫千佛经。一一佛于因地遇佛时。皆先以财宝乃至柳枝净水等世尊供养。然后发菩提心。悲华经。宝海梵志。劝无量人天发菩提心。先令以物献佛。然后启愿。佛佛道同。故须导禀。）	（準賢劫千佛經。一一佛於因地遇佛時。皆先以財寶乃至柳枝淨水等世尊供養。然後發菩提心。悲華經。寶海梵志。勸無量人天發菩提心。先令以物獻佛。然後啟願。佛佛道同。故須導禀。）
启发之后。念念运心。便为成佛正因。宜自深加喜庆。道俗不乖于法侣。山川岂碍真智。幸因路人垂示姓字。开成三年六月二十日绵州刺史裴休记。	啟發之後。念念運心。便為成佛正因。宜自深加喜慶。道俗不乖於法侶。山川豈礙真智。幸因路人垂示姓字。開成三年六月二十日綿州刺史裴休記。
劝发菩提心文。（终）	勸發菩提心文。（終）

requested that one first relinquish some form of material wealth in a manner befitting one's abilities to do so. In some cases it may be appropriate to pool one's resources and use them in making offerings to the Triple Jewel. In other cases, one may choose to create a painting of an image or choose to devote energetic service to the operation of the *bodhimaṇḍala*. Then, afterwards, one may rely upon this essay proper as one earnestly brings forth the great vows.

> **Interlinear note:** According to the *Sutra of the Thousand Buddhas of the Auspicious Kalpa*, in each and every case where a buddha on the causal ground encountered a buddha, he would in all cases use material wealth or jewels or even such things as a willow branch and pure water in first making an offering to the Bhagavān. Afterwards, he would then bring forth the bodhi resolve.
>
> In the *Flower of Compassion Sutra*, the Brahmacārin, Jeweled Sea, encouraged countless men and gods to generate the bodhi resolve, first influencing them to utilize some object as an offering to the Buddha. Then, afterwards, they would announce their vows. From buddha to buddha, the path is identical. Therefore, it is essential to honor this request.

After communicating the generation [of the bodhi resolve], one should invoke that resolve in each and every thought. This will then constitute a correct cause for the realization of buddhahood. It is only appropriate that one should then feel profound sentiments of joyful felicitation. Neither monastics nor laity should allow themselves to become estranged from Dharma friends. How could even mountains or rivers [be allowed to] present an obstacle to [the realization of] genuine wisdom?[59]

This man possessed of fortunate causal affinities here leaves behind his name: Written out by District Magistrate Peixiu in Mianzhou on the twentieth day of the sixth month of the third year of the Kaicheng reign period (839 CE).[60]

End of *An Exhortation to Resolve on Buddhahood*

Part Three Endnotes

1. This "turtle-mirror" (*guijing*:龜鏡), although seemingly obscure, is a traditional literary idiom signifying an exemplary standard and guide for the correct and wise actions of future generations. The basis for its wording lies in the legendary reliability of the turtle-shell oracle for divination and in the accuracy of a mirror's reflection of the beauty or grotesqueness of the present situation.

2. There is a scribal error here in the *Xuzang* edition of the Canon (henceforth: "XZ") which substitutes a graphically similar glyph for the *dan* (但) which means "only; solely." Although obvious in any case, this is verified by my woodblock edition (henceforth, simply "WB"), originally carved as one fascicle of a *Buddhist Middle School Lesson Book* (佛教中學課本). Although WB is most likely of late-Qing provenance, its actual origin is unknown to me.

3. The quoted text is from the preface to the Book of Songs (詩經).

4. "Great Community" is a formal term of reference for any particular congregation of Buddhists meeting at the same place or for all of the disciples of a particular spiritual guide. In more abstract contexts, it may even be intended to refer to all Buddhists within a given tradition or national cultural frame.

5. "Same lineage" likely refers specifically to traditions sharing the same Great Vehicle doctrinal tenets as opposed to one wherein individual liberation is esteemed over universal liberation.

6. The character which I render as "pathway" (趣) is the one typically used to refer to "realm of rebirth," this being an indication that the maker of such a vow would tend to disdain merely luxuriating in celestial rebirths, even if his stock of merit was more than adequate for taking on such a birth at the conclusion of this present human life. The implication is that one would vow instead to continue cultivating the Bodhisattva Path in the realms of existence more obviously freighted with suffering.

7. The "Dragon Flower Assembly" is the congregation of beings for whom Maitreya (the next buddha) shall proclaim the Dharma.

8. *Li* 理 = noumenon = emptiness. Hence the meaning of "right" is "knowing which accords with things as they really are in their very essence." This circularity of terminology finds its origin in the Chinese *Avataṃsaka* School's use of this *li* to connote the Indian Buddhist concept of "emptiness."

8. WB: Scribal error in XZ, erroneously recording *rong* (容) where it should be the graphically-similar *ke* (客).

9. WB: XZ substitutes the scribal error *zhi* (智) for the clearly intended

zhi (知). This is easily deducible from examining the previous line of text.

10. "Cuts off the hundred sorts of fallacies" (絕百非) is a reference to a stock phrase: "transcends the four propositions (the "tetralemma" [*catuṣ-pāda, catuṣ-koṭi*]) and cuts off the hundred fallacies" (離四句絕百非). This is usually descriptive of ultimate truth's leaving behind the fallacies inherent in the sphere of conventional truth's conceptuality-bound frames of reference.

11. This is a quote from the 60-fascicle edition of the *Avataṃsaka Sutra* translated by Buddhabhadra (T09.278.465c). As phrased in that scripture, it reads, "The mind, the Buddha, and beings as well—in these three, there are no distinctions." (心佛及眾生，是三無差別).

12. XZ introduces a scribal error throughout the entire text by employing duo-decimal cycle character *si* (巳) for what should be *ji* (己) which is a self-referent.

13. This appears to be a paraphrase from fascicle six of the *Śūraṅgama Sūtra* (*Da fo ding rulai mi yin xiu zheng liao yi zhu pusa wan heng shoulengyan jing* – 大佛頂如來密因修證了義諸菩薩萬行首楞嚴經 [T19.945.131c]).

14. This is an abbreviated sentence from section seven (the "selflessness" section) of the *Laozi* which in full reads: "聖人後其身而身先."

15. The four means (lit. "dharmas") of attraction (*catuḥ-saṃgraha-vastu*) are: giving, pleasing words, beneficial actions, and [accompaniment in] mutual endeavors.

16. WB: XZ introduces another scribal error by substituting "wisdom" (*zhi*: 智) where the character should be "compassion" (*bei*: 悲). This is obvious anyway from the nature of the rational sequiturs.

17. I have preferred here the alternate reading of *lian* (練) from the woodblock edition to the *bao* (寶) of XZ which contradicts both intuition and correct syntax.

18. This is a reference to the 10,000 subsidiary practices perfected by all buddhas (along with the six perfections) as prerequisites for realization of the utmost, right, and perfect enlightenment of a buddha.

19. WB: Another corruption in XZ. The character for "wick" (*zhu*: 炷) has been accidentally dropped.

20. This is a passage from the 40-fascicle Tang Dynasty translation of the *Gandavyuha* made under imperial auspices by the Kashmiri Tripiṭaka Master Prajñā (T10.293.846c).

21. The four immeasurable minds (*apramāṇacitta*) are kindness, compassion, sympathetic joy, and equanimity.

22. The six pāramitās are giving, moral virtue, patience, vigor, meditative skill, and transcendental wisdom.

23. The splendid youth Sudhana is the protagonist of the *Gandavyuha* section of the *Avataṃsaka Sutra* wherein he progressively interviews fifty-three good spiritual guides, culminating with his encounter with the great bodhisattva, Samantabhadra.

24. "The Two Vehicles" refers to: 1) the path of the Śrāvakas or "Hearer-disciples" which culminates in arhatship, and 2) the path of the Pratyekabuddhas (those who awaken in the absence of a buddha through contemplation of the twelve links in the chain of causality) which culminates in a somewhat more refined level of awakening. Although the nirvāṇa realized by arhats and pratyekabuddhas does not differ appreciably from that gained by buddhas, the actual level of knowledges and awakening cherished among practitioners of the Two Vehicles is not even remotely comparable to the utmost, right, and perfect enlightenment realized only by buddhas.

    Although the vast majority of spiritual cultivation techniques pursued by Two Vehicles' practitioners are held in common with Great Vehicle practitioners, the arhat and pratyekabuddha paths themselves are not encouraged in Mahāyāna Buddhism because they focus solely on individual liberation and hence are not much concerned with the liberation of other beings.

25. "Jeweled Sea" was a previous bodhisattvic incarnation of Shākyamuni Buddha.

26. WB: XZ apparently corrupts the text through substitution of a graphically similar character (*cui*: 摧) which can only be made sensible by resort to an obscure classical definition "to stoop down." The woodblock edition preserves a very standard and intuitively appropriate binome employing what is obviously the more correct glyph (*qüan xiao*: 權小).

27. "Provisional" refers to teachings not directly revealing ultimate reality. These were employed by the Buddha to gradually raise a disciple's understanding out of the blatantly false views of the foolish common person.

    "Lesser-scope" refers to teachings which, if followed to their endpoints, would lead to non-ultimate results such as arhatship or pratyekabuddhahood.

28. "Flowers floating in space" is an idiom referring to the subjective visual impression created by tiny bits of matter floating around on the surface of one's eyeballs which are sometimes mistakenly perceived as external phenomena. This is a metaphor for the false imputations which the deluded mind places on the objective data perceivable by the eye, ear, nose, tongue, body, and intellectual mind. The meaning of "illusional obscurations" is similar: The external phenomena are devoid of any inherent existence of their own. Nonetheless, our

delusion-based perceptive imperfections construct false imputations about them.

29. WB: XZ seems to insert a redundant "great" glyph (*da*: 大).

30. "The two extreme [views]" refers to annihilationism and eternalism.

31. This is an alternate glyph for the *tang* (倘) which here simply means "if" or "in the event that."

32. *Beihua jing*: 悲華經 (T3.157.198b-c).

33. Short for *shutimona* (樹提摩納), a figure prominent in the *Flower of Compassion Sutra* (*Beihua jing* – 悲華經). This is a mostly-continuous citation from fascicle five of that scripture (T3.157.198b-c).

34. Both WB and XB commit the error of substituting "immeasurable" for the "inexhaustible" used in Dharmarakṣa's translation of the sutra as well as in the names of the four list components. I have restored it to agree with the original and to resolve the contradiction between list title and list names (T3.157.198b).

35. "Giving" is one of the four means of attraction employed by the bodhisattva in influencing beings to become amenable to receiving teaching.

36. The five hindrances (*nīvaraṇa*), also known as the five "coverings" (*āvaraṇa*), are: "sensual desire," or simply "desire" (*kāmacchanda*); "ill will" (*vyāpāda*); "lethargy-and-sleepiness" (*styāna-middha*); "excited-ness-and-regretfulness" (*auddhatya-kaukṛtya*); and "afflicted doubtful-ness" (*vicikitsā*).

37. An *araṇya* is a remote dwelling intended for solitary cultivation, espe-cially solitary meditation practice.

38. The basic standard categories involved in the stations of mindfulness involve regarding the body as unlovely, feelings as conducing to suf-fering, thoughts as impermanent, and dharmas (i.e. "phenomena") as non-self.

39. The four right efforts involve severing already-arisen karmic unwhole-someness, guarding against not-yet-arisen karmic unwholesomeness, generating not-yet-arisen karmic good, and bringing about growth of already-arisen karmic good.

40. A mildly obscure list, the four bases of psychic power vary in their iterations. A common standard listing: zeal (*chanda*), single-minded-ness (*citta*), vigor (*vīrya*), and deep mental reflection (*mīmāṃsā-samādhi-prahāṇa*).

41. The five root-faculties (*indriya*) are: faith, vigor, mindfulness, con-centration, and wisdom. The five powers which here follow on the heels of the five root-faculties bear the precisely the same component names. Why? It is because they are simply a more perfectly developed

stage of the same path components. Hence, in their less-developed form, they are merely faculties which have not yet realized their full potential. In their more-developed form, they have become fully ripened powers possessed of the power to destroy all afflictions.

42. The reader may notice that I have reconstructed from the sutra text in the *Taisho* canon a missing 15-character phrase (shown in brackets in the English and below in this endnote) which was lost from Peixiu's text in both the WB and XZ editions.

In the absence of this restoration, the corruption had achieved the effect of grafting the predicate of the subsequent sentence onto the subject of the preceding sentence, thus corrupting the intended meaning of both sentences. The two sentences of interest are: 諸根即是助菩提法。攝取諸根成就故。諸力即是助菩提法。摧滅一切煩惱故。(T3.157.198c)

When the missing fragment of *Taisho* text states, "...because, on account of them, one consolidates the faculties...," it means that it is the training in the five faculties themselves which enhances and fortifies these faculties and eventually elevates them to the level of "five powers." Of course it may also be making a peripheral reference to other path-related faculties as well.

43. The seven limbs of enlightenment (*bodhi-aṅga*) are: dharma selection, vigor, joy, lightness-and-peacefulness (*praśrabdhi*), mindfulness, concentration, and equanimity within the sphere of the compositional-factor aggregate (*saṃskāra-upekṣā*).

44. The six harmonies, typically matters of greatest concern for denizens of monastic communities, are harmony as regards: body, mouth, mind, precepts, views, and the accrual of benefits.

45. WB and *Taisho*: XZ corrupts through dropping the word "path" (*dao*: 道).

46. The name translation here (Vijaya = "victory") is somewhat conjectural. Note that XZ corrupts the name through scribal error. It is in fact correctly recorded as 毘舍耶無垢 in this passage from the very same sutra just quoted at length in the preceding section of this text. (T3.157.201a)

47. Note that the original scripture text as recorded in *Taisho* speaks more to the motivation of the vows: "...are *not done for the sake of* training and subduing of beings.... " (T3.157.201a).

48. One will note that XZ introduces another scribal error which the woodblock edition does not commit: that of naming the source text incorrectly as the *Flower of Kindness Sutra*.

49. Only dropping a few phrases from the source text, Peixiu continues on here to quote from the *Flower of Compassion Sutra*. (T3.157.201a-b)

50. XZ introduces another scribal error by substituting for the *chi* (持) of

both *Taisho* and WB the graphically similar, but clearly erroneous *she* (捨).

51. This entire section devoted to the merit involved in generating the bodhi mind consists of selected passages sequentially extracted from the *Floral Adornment (Avataṃsaka) Sutra's* Chapter Seventeen: "The Merit from the Initial Generation of the Bodhi Mind" (T10.89a-91c).

    This edition of the sutra is a translation of the 80-fascicle edition brought to Luoyang in 695 CE by the Khotanese tripiṭaka master Śikṣānanda who served as the primary translator, assisted by Bodhiruci and Yijing. This translator data according to *Foguang Dictionary*: 5784c-a.

52. When comparing with the *Taisho* sutra text, it is apparent that both WB and XZ abbreviate away four comparisons, XZ adds an extra *koṭī* (億) on the end which I drop in this translation, and both WB and XZ add in an extra phrase: 百萬那由他億分 ("...one part in a million *nayutas* of *koṭīs*..." which I *do* translate here.

    Now as regards these Sanskrit number categories, see the following:

    A *nayuta* is a numeral explained variously as "one hundred thousand," "one million," or "ten million." (This according to Soothill's dictionary.)

    A *koṭī* is *also* explained variously as "one hundred thousand," "one million," or "ten million." (This *also* according to Soothill.)

    As for an *upaniṣad*, it is the most extreme measure of minuteness in Sanskrit numerology and is a measure of subatomic minuteness "bordering on emptiness" which at its very largest would appear to be represented, as a trillionth part of a trillionth part of a hair (sic). This would appear to involve, in decimal-fraction terms a "one" placed twenty-five positions to the right of the decimal?

    The recipe is arrived at as follows: First one takes a hair and chops it into a hundred parts. Then one takes one of those hundred parts and chops it into ten billion parts. (We're now at a trillionth part of a hair.) Next, divide one of those parts to the same degree once again until you arrive at a particle "bordering on emptiness." This would seem to bring us down to (at most) "a trillionth part of a trillionth part." This is my interpretation of the matter as reported in *Foguang Dictionary* (FG.5684c) of Huiyüan's Sanskrit Glossary (*yinyi*) drawing upon the *Great Yogacara Śāstra*.

53. An immeasurably large number.

54. The ten wholesome karmic deeds (*kuśala-karma*) consist in not committing the ten bad karmic deeds. These consist of three related to physical karma (killing, stealing, sexual misconduct), four related to verbal karma (false speech, harsh speech, duplicitous or divisive

speech, frivolous speech [including "lewd" speech]), and three related to mental karma (covetousness, anger, incorrect views).

Careful adherence to these ten standards of moral virtue have the karmic effect of conducing to celestial rebirth unless the merit deriving therefrom is "transferred" through dedicating it to the utmost, right, and perfect enlightenment of buddhahood.

55. This refers to a "first-stage arhat," otherwise known as a "stream-enterer."

56. This refers to a "second-stage" arhat, otherwise known as a "once-returner."

57. This refers to a "third-stage" arhat, otherwise known as a "never-returner."

58. It is fairly clear that this interlinear note was inserted to prevent undue grandiosity and self-delusion on the part of the enthusiastic new convert to the Bodhisattva Path. It might do us well to reflect at some length on the differences between a mere "facsimile" generation of the bodhi mind typical of the good-hearted foolish common person and the genuinely perfect generation of the bodhi mind more typical of a journeyman bodhisattva. The issues surrounding this difference are explored in a very inspiring way in the following section.

59. XZ has dropped the preposition 夫 which is nicely preserved in WB. This is obvious because the two sentences are written in matched couplet style (道俗不乖於法侶。山川豈礙夫真智。)

60. Peixiu refers to himself as a "district magistrate" at the end of his exhortation whereas the text refers to him in the author-credit line as "prime minister." This is because Peixiu's rise to the more exalted governmental station occurred some years after he authored this exhortation.

About the Translator

Bhikshu Dharmamitra (ordination name "Heng Shou"– 釋恆授) is a Chinese-tradition translator-monk and one of the early American disciples (since 1968) of the late Weiyang Ch'an patriarch, Dharma teacher, and exegete, the Venerable Master Hsuan Hua (宣化上人). He has a total of 23 years in robes during two periods as a monastic (1969–1975; 1991 to present).

Dharmamitra's principal educational foundations as a translator lie in four years of intensive monastic training and Chinese-language study of classic Mahāyāna texts in a small-group setting under Master Hua from 1968–1972, undergraduate Chinese language study at Portland State University, a year of intensive one-on-one Classical Chinese study at the Fu Jen University Language Center near Taipei, and two years at the University of Washington's School of Asian Languages and Literature (1988–90).

Since taking robes again under Master Hua in 1991, Dharmamitra has devoted his energies primarily to study and translation of classic Mahāyāna texts with a special interest in works by Ārya Nāgārjuna and related authors. To date, he has translated a dozen important texts, most of which are slated for publication by Kalavinka Press.

Kalavinka Buddhist Classics Title List

Meditation Instruction Texts

The Essentials of Buddhist Meditation
A marvelously complete classic *śamathā-vipaśyanā* (calming-and-insight) meditation manual. By Tiantai Śramaṇa Zhiyi (538–597 CE).

Six Gates to the Sublime
The earliest Indian Buddhist meditation method explaining the essentials of breath and calming-and-insight meditation. By Śramaṇa Zhiyi.

Bodhisattva Path Texts

Nāgārjuna on the Six Perfections
Chapters 17–30 of Ārya Nāgārjuna's *Mahāprājñāpāramitā Upadeśa*.

Marvelous Stories from the Perfection of Wisdom
130 Stories from Ārya Nāgārjuna's *Mahāprājñāpāramitā Upadeśa*.

A Strand of Dharma Jewels (Ārya Nāgārjuna's *Ratnāvalī*)
The earliest extant edition, translated by Paramārtha: *ca* 550 CE

Nāgārjuna's Guide to the Bodhisattva Path
The *Bodhisaṃbhāra Treatise* with abridged Vaśitva commentary.

The Bodhisaṃbhāra Treatise Commentary
The complete exegesis by the Indian Bhikshu Vaśitva (*ca* 300–500 CE).

Letter from a Friend - The Three Earliest Editions
The earliest extant editions of Ārya Nāgārjuna's *Suhṛlekkha*:

Translated by Tripiṭaka Master Guṇavarman	(*ca* 425 CE)
Translated by Tripiṭaka Master Saṅghavarman	(*ca* 450 CE)
Translated by Tripiṭaka Master Yijing	(*ca* 675 CE)

Resolve-for-Enlightenment Texts

On Generating the Resolve to Become a Buddha
On the Resolve to Become a Buddha by Ārya Nāgārjuna
Exhortation to Resolve on Buddhahood by Patriarch Sheng'an Shixian
Exhortation to Resolve on Buddhahood by the Tang Literatus, Peixiu

Vasubandhu's Treatise on Resolving to Become a Buddha
By Vasubandhu Bodhisattva (*ca* 300 CE)

*All Kalavinka Press translations include facing-page source text.